COUNSELING OUR OWN

LESBIAN/GAY SUBCULTURE MEETS THE MENTAL HEALTH SYSTEM

CHARNA KLEIN

First Printing 1986

Although the author and publisher made an effort to verify the facts contained in this book, we cannot guarantee all are correct. The author and publisher assume no responsibility for errors, inaccuracies, omissions or any inconsistency herein. Any slights of people or organizations are unintentional.

ISBN 0-9617216-0-X

Design and Production   **Publication Service, Inc.**
Lance Taylor Design   **Renton, WA 98055**
(206) 243-3278   **(206) 228-5240**

TABLE
OF CONTENTS

ACKNOWLEDGEMENTS: I wish to thank
the staff and clients of the gay counseling services
and gay communities in the United States and the
following persons in particular from Seattle Counseling
Services for Sexual Minorities: Dr. Robert Deisher,
Sandra Fosshage, Patricia Kalafus, Gwyn Hanscom,
and Charles Strago. I thank Joan de Foreest for her
help with the national survey of gay counseling
services. I thank Margaret Dougherty and Publication
Service, Inc. for typesetting services. Finally, I thank
the following persons who helped me with the
preparation of the manuscript and personally:
Dr. Kenneth E. Read, Dr. Sue-Ellen Jacobs,
Dr. Robert Kus, Robert Wall, Ann Manly, M. Moore,
and J.F. Special thanks go to Judith Winter for
help in organizing, editing, troubleshooting, and for
"tracking with" me.

This book is dedicated to the millions of
lesbian women and gay men,
as well as women, ethnic and racial
minorities, struggling to be themselves
in a world which denies and opposes this.

The author has a background as a psychological and medical anthropologist. She worked at Seattle Counseling Service for seven years. She is currently a writer, teacher, and consultant. She has trained many mental health professionals in ethnotherapy and ethnomedicine—in how to work with cultural, racial and sexual differences between professional practitioner and client.

PREFACE

This book deals with a subject many do not want to deal with in the open or at all. I've written under my own name and not a pen-name. This is authentic. This makes a statement of refusal to submit to the forces of fear, the cover-up, the lie. However, individuals' names are not used in the book. Why should they not be? Why should the point even come up.

Were we living in a different world—one in which it was not considered a crime, sickness, culturally, socially, and familially objectionable, or even subtly gauche to be gay or to discuss the subject—this would be unnecessary. Were we in a different world gays would feel more free to discuss and be more open about who they are.

Sadly, we live in a world where there are closed doors, where people feel compelled to hide who they are and what they feel. We live in a world in which people are denied the basic civil and human rights, where people lose jobs, housing, families, community, for being openly who they are. We live in a world in which people are afraid to love.

This book is my contribution to opening the doors for difference. If the doors were already open, this book would not be necessary.

My Rainbow Dance

By Ariella Myerson

I have ploughed my fields of grief
Ripping up the earth
Chopping down the stubborn trunks
Of dead trees, in my mind;
I will vomit out my anger...
Rake away my rage...
Sow my fields with hope and joy
Seasoned with my rain;
Stormy clouds blow past my mind...
Blocking out the sun
Rainbow colors laugh with me
And dance away my pain.

CHAPTER 1

"It is a phenomenal act of courage and self assertion to accept and own a part of oneself that society says is 'sick' and you know inside it is not, and you are not, and you are the only authority for that decision."

— Sybil Meyer, Therapist

WHAT IS COUNSELING?

Before there were gay counseling services, troubled gay persons might be seen in psychiatrists' offices and mental institutions or talking to friends, and they still are. Others talked to the bartender—the proverbial ear for hardship stories—or sat quietly in the bar talking to no one and they still do. They also sat at home and talked to no one.

Beginning in 1969, gays had another choice: the Seattle Counseling Service for Sexual Minorities.[1] The Seattle Counseling Service (SCS) was the first of its kind. Other such services have since developed all over the country.

Clients who sought counseling at SCS were asked to evaluate services they had previously received at non-gay counseling services.[2] They answered the question, "Did you experience any problems in counseling based on your sex, sexual orientation or gender identity? If yes, please state where and what was involved." Forty-eight percent responded that they had difficulty finding appropriate counseling. They made comments such as:

> My M.D. had no idea that gender identity problems really exist. When I talked with him, he was cold

3

and distant. He recommended I seek psychiatric help.

I was in need of the tools to accept myself as the caring, sensitive gay man I am, not therapy that was aimed at making me into a straight man.

Many clients had been referred to Seattle Counseling Service for Sexual Minorities by a friend, a lover, a lesbian/gay or health care agency, a non-gay agency or health care provider, or through an advertisement.

Some clients state specific reasons related to SCS resources and programs, that SCS is specialized for sexual minorities, or the desire to talk with another lesbian or gay person. Many of the answers have to do with a sense of trust, comfort, identity and positive sense of being understood and cared for. Some clients state a fear of homophobic reaction elsewhere. Clients made comments like:

It helped me look at myself and see a human. I'm homosexual, and my problems are relating to this.

I really needed help upon my arrival here. I didn't have any friends, no job and feeling quite hopeless.

Brought me back to reality.

SCS has helped me tremendously — both through the contacts in the community that it gave me...contacts of people and places supportive of my lifestyle.

My wife and I are talking to each other more than we did in ten years of marriage. [3]

In response to the question, "Do you perceive a need for mental health agencies specifically for sexual minorities," 94% answered "yes."

> Sexuality of any kind is still taboo for many people and one of the most difficult things to talk about. Having a specific agency for counseling helps.

> It's a lot easier to go in and get help when you know you won't be condemned for who or what you are.

> There are a variety of unique situations encountered by sexual minorities. Of course their larger life situation is much like anyone else's but some specialized help is essential.

These clients have shown a highly positive response to SCS. Seventy-two percent evaluated SCS as "excellent" and an additional 27% rated it as "good."

They have commented:

> I think it's nice to know there are people who care about sexual minorities and are willing to be there to listen and talk about your problems.

> SCS has given me new hope for my gay life and has helped me to realize that I am human too. I have feelings and they're important. I also feel the government needs to help us educate the public by working with us.

Clients have told their own thoughts and feelings in their own words. Their comments are surely the most telling testimony of the need for and raison d'etre of lesbian/gay counseling services.

The matter of sexual preference vocabulary has been one of this author's more bothersome concerns.

The term "gay" nowadays seems to be construed as only applying to gay men, and the term "lesbian" of course refers to the women. It used to be that "gay" meant both the women and the men who had a same-sex preference. The term "homosexual" had been dropped from the subcultural dictionary. It was considered to be overly clinical and associated with biased writing. That was before women realized that homosexual men—like their heterosexual counterparts—could and did discriminate and devalue women.

It was also clear that everyone—from male researchers to men in media, business, etc.—meant "gay men" when they referred to "gays." Many lesbians chose to distinguish themselves from gay men and male perceptions, ways and associations. They adopted for themselves the term "lesbian," based on the Greek Isle of Lesbos where poetess Sappho and her friends held their love-in. The term "lesbian" became popular when the women's movement's influence was felt. This writer is attempting to be politically correct by distinguishing the terms "gay" and "lesbian"—and also write a smooth-flowing prose. "Lesbian/gay" or "gay/lesbian"— and it does matter which one you use—is cumbersome. This author sometimes uses the "lesbian/gay" formulation. At other times simply the shorter term, "gay" is used, which is meant to describe both women and men. Sometimes the terms "male gays" and "gay men" are used to refer specifically to male homosexuals. The term "gay women" is also used. It doesn't make good sense for women to give up the term "gay." This author doesn't believe that women should surrender to men once common territory. This territory can be words as well as places and institutions. The term "gay" is a good way to talk about issues that lesbians and male gays share. Besides, "gay" is a rather nice, short, easily-used word. The author hopes that for these reasons women will not be offended and turned off by the use of the word "gay."

While most of the material in this book applies to lesbians and gay men, their subculture, movement and institutions, a wider population of "sexual minorities" is also discussed.

Who are the "sexual minorities"? This term is used to cover a grouping of sexual and genderal categories, which constitute a minority in numbers relative to the total population, whose members suffer social-cultural nonrecognition and stigmatization. The term is not applied to sexual practices per se[4] but to personal gender identity and the choice of sex of one's partner. Certainly there are heterosexuals and homosexuals who have varying sexual practices, which are not contingent on sexual orientation or gender identity.

Sexual minorities will refer to homosexuals, male and female, bisexuals, transvestites and transsexuals (who we also term transgenderal, since the primary distinguishing criteria is gender not sex). It is not the goal here to delve into the complicated considerations of definitional criteria, such as self-identification and definition, feelings, behaviors, frequency and exclusivity of sexual contacts, changeability of sexuality and sexual identification, etc. Oftentimes these facets are inconsistent in persons, for examples, someone who frequently engages in sex with (a) member(s) of the same sex but does not consider her/himself as being homosexual, or a person who has never had homosexual relations who may identify as a homosexual.

The following descriptive terms will give the reader an understanding of who are sexual minorities referred to in this book:

sexual orientation—This term refers to the partner preference with whom one has or would have sexual relations. It encompasses heterosexual, homosexual, and bisexual orientations. Heterosexual is the cultural and statistical norm and is not considered as a sexual minority category.

bisexual — This term refers to sexual orientation to both one's own and one's opposite sex. Bisexual persons are considered to be outside of the cultural norm, although it is sometimes suggested that we are all or the majority of persons are bisexual or would be bisexual if it were not for societal constraints, socialization, or channeling into either homosexuality or heterosexuality.

homosexual/lesbian/gay—These terms refer to individuals who have a sexual orientation or preference for individuals of the same sex. The terms "homosexual" or "gay" are usually applied to males and "lesbian" to females. However, the term "gay" is often used and will refer to both female and male homosexuals. The term "lesbian" will refer to female homosexuals.

non-sexual, asexual—"Non-sexual" means no sexual activity. "Asexual" is defined biologically. In its application to people, asexual can be said to include absence of sex identity or orientation as well as activity.

gender identity—This term refers to that social and anatomical gender which a person conceives him/herself to be; being recognized as this self definition with the pronoun "he" or "she." There are also persons who see themselves as both male and female simultaneously or at different times. Then again, there can be people who see themselves as neither. The term gender identity includes males, females, and transgenderals.

transgenderal/transsexual—These terms refer to biologically described males and females whose psychological orientation, their gender identity, lies with the other gender. These individuals are those who, at times, may surgically have their external biological sex changed to fit with their psychologic identification.

transvestite—This term refers to persons who assume the dress of the opposite sex, a man who wears women's clothing for example, as a significant aspect of that person's sexuality. This includes male, female, heterosexual and homosexual persons but in the vast number of instances, occurs in male heterosexuals.

Sexual orientation, gender identity, and culturally defined masculine and feminine roles are viewed as analytically separate aspects. These aspects may or may not overlap in any preconceived, consistent pattern along male and female biological or cultural lines in actual persons. A case in point illustrative of the separateness of these factors is that of a person who has had a sex change operation from male to female, who is a lesbian in sexual orientation, and who does not exercise traditional feminine role patterns in terms of dress and demeanor.

What must be recognized, in all this, is that sexual identification is broad and varied. The culturally-accepted definition of two distinct, male and female genders, with heterosexual orientation, and appropriate masculine and feminine role behaviors represents a small part of the actual variation in sexual identity. The best known and reliable source of the numbers of persons who are gay or lesbian are the Alfred Kinsey studies of 1948 and 1953 on the human male and female. According to these studies, generally 10% of the population is actively gay. The figures differ somewhat for men and women. Thirty-seven percent of males and 18% of females reported an overt experience to orgasm, and 50% of males and 28% of females reported an erotic response to members of the same sex.

Figures for bisexuality, transsexualism and transvestism are less well known. Pauley estimated figures for female transsexualism (change from a male to a female): "The prevalence of female transsexualism has been estimated at from 1 in 103,000 in Sweden to 1 in 400,000 in the United States."[5] Ira Pauley points out that these figures are on the low side since they refer only to those who report to the medical profession in requesting medical intervention. Figures for male transsexualism (change from female to male) are lacking. Seemingly the change from female to male is less common than that from male to female.

This is borne out by the experience at Seattle Counseling Service. Several other factors might be involved according to Pauley: greater publicity given to male transsexualism so that the public is more aware that such an option exists; and the availability of more advanced surgical techniques in dealing with female transsexualism as compared with male transsexualism.[6] Pauley suggests that perhaps more male transsexuals might come forth if the surgical procedures have more to offer them. Another explanation hypothesized by Kinsey is that 'the male is more prone to conditioning by psychological stimuli in the sexual and gender sphere than is the female.'[7]

Transvestism is seemingly more frequent than is transsexualism. It has been estimated at 1200 to 1600 in King County, with a population of 1,231,000, or about one in 879 persons. Transvestites often call on the telephone to discuss this issue and appear less often in person.

Sexual behavior and identity do not always coincide. Schwartz and Blumstein[8] note that more people are behaviorally bisexual than so identify.[9] This disparity is no doubt associated with the stigmatized status of homosexuality.

Lesbians and gay men have been branded in our culture as "sick," "evil," and "criminal." They have been labeled "deviant." Deviance creates boundaries between what is acceptable and unacceptable. The deviant is outside the pale of acceptable society.

Two stigmas are attached to lesbians and gay men: sexual preference and being labeled mentally ill. Dr. Phyllis Vine, an historian of health care and teacher of health advocacy, defines stigma as "based on a culture's consensus that a certain attribute is inherently unworthy... it may be any characteristic that is used to differentiate those who are socially acceptable from those who are not."[10] Dr. Vine explains the dysfunctionality of stigma: "Stigma is society's means of protecting itself against falsely conceived dangers. In doing so, it legitimizes ridicule, humiliation and dehumanization of persons with emotional problems."[11]

As elements of gay subculture consciously rejected cultural views regarding sexual deviancy, the need grew for a gay mental health delivery system based on the premise that gays have legitimate mental health needs and that gayness itself is not a sickness. The need grew for practitioners who did not presume sin, crime or illness, nor admonish their gay clients to take a more "normal" place on the bell curve of sexual preference.

Bill Owen of the University of California in San Francisco, wrote an article about gay sexual practices in relation to health problems specific to men. The mental or medical care provider to lesbians and gay men can "best help their homosexual (clients) by accepting them and their relationships nonjudgmentally and by understanding their special (mental) health needs,"[12] according to Dr. Owen.

They have been called dykes, faggots, fence-sitters, queers and queens. These are the sexual minorities...the homosexuals, bisexuals, transsexuals, and transvestites. They have been viewed as criminals, sinners, and mentally ill. How do they deal with these labels? Who provides an empathetic ear and helping hand?

These are the questions dealt with in this book. The purpose is to describe and analyze the development, nature, role and results of the specialized, gay counseling services and the larger subcultural and cultural contexts in which they are embedded. They sprang up in response to felt needs for positive services by gay people. This need was not being met by the established mental health system. Thus a parallel, alternative system of gay counseling services arose. They gained some credibility with the larger mental health system and in some cases, became associated with it.

The first of these services began in 1969 in Seattle, Washington, followed by others around the country. They developed out of a peculiar set of historical forces, including the era of the 1960s and the gay and mental health movements.

The understanding of gay counseling services nationally is deepened by an historical ethnography of the Seattle Service as an institution, its staff and clients, and interrelations with the local gay community and mental health system.

The data and analyses build a broad understanding of gay people and mental health, the counseling service and gay subculture, and the role of gay people as agents of change in relationship to the larger socio-cultural system. We conclude with a statement about mental health and culture and the need for an ethnomedical model, recommendations, and suggestions for therapists, students, planners and administrators.

Different types of services appeal to different individuals. The decentralization and variety of services in some cities allows for these differences in consumer interests to be met.

In Seattle, the services are oriented to social and community concerns and to mental health concerns in varying degrees in different agencies. The Los Angeles model of a centralized, comprehensive mental health and gay community center is clearly different from a mental health oriented service such as the Institute for Human Identity or the Chicago Counseling and Psychotherapy Center. These different types of services appeal to different individuals. The decentralization and variety of services in some cities allows for these differences in consumer interests to be met.

Some clients mistrust all professionals, associating them with the traditional medical model of sexual minorities as sick. According to the medical model, personal problems are rooted in an individual problem or pathology rather than in a social-cultural problem. This places the onus of illness on the individual gay person. Many gay people have seen through and rejected this model. Other clients mistrust peer counselors, seeing them as inadequately prepared to deal with mental health problems—and prefer to work with professionals.

Gay counseling centers differ in the professional, para-professional and non-professional status of their staff. The Gay Community Services Center in Los Angeles has a peer counseling approach. No attempt is made to be professional therapists. There is an in-house, peer counselor training program. The Center's staff are not interested in "Curing" people and avoid use of terms such as "patient," "client," "therapy," and others that are part of a traditional medical model. They were cautious in accepting professional practitioners committed to practicing the medical model. All staff were

13

expected to function as peers to counselees. Counselors were also invariably sexual minorities, giving clients options for choosing a counselor of a similar background.

In contrast to GCSC, New York's Institute for Human Identity is oriented to professional therapy. The issue of peer versus professional counseling was instrumental in its formation and controversial in the development of gay counseling services in New York. Identity House offered the peer counseling alternative.

Para- and non-professional counseling has been referred to as "peer counseling." The philosophy behind peer counseling is that persons who are on a par and share similar life experiences can most comfortably and effectively relate to one another in a therapeutic situation. This is especially applicable to minority, stigmatized people, such as women, racial and sexual minorities. These people have traditionally not found help from people who are or who are felt to be, their oppressors. In the case of women, especially, counselors who are white, male, and heterosexual pose a problem. Women and sexual minorities have often been invalidated and exploited by therapists. The argument for peer counseling is sound in this respect. Studies have found therapeutic outcome to be similar for peer and professional counselors. Peer counselors usually recognize their limitations and refer clients to professional therapists when necessary, and peer counseling centers refer as a matter of course.

In addition to varying client preferences for peer or professional counselors, there is the issue of sexual preference of counselors. It is generally recognized in the gay community that gay counselors are more likely than non-gay counselors to be accepting and supportive of gayness, that this may be a problem for non-gay counselors. Nevertheless, it is usually not ruled out that there are non-gay persons who overcome homophobia and are good, empathetic counselors for gay persons. One center attempted to balance its staff with gay and non-gay counselors.

The centers all have a client-centered approach to counseling. The Chicago center is actually an outgrowth and continuation of the counseling center founded by Carl Rogers at the University of Chicago in 1945. Their philosophy is consonant with labeling theory discussed in chapter 3 of this book. Their approach, generally applicable to gay counseling services, is based on: "In the client-centered tradition...the labels 'sick' and 'abnormal' are considered inappropriate and harmful to the client's psychological well being...It is necessary to work with clients' own definitions of their problems and to facilitate the discovery and use of their own resources for personal growth and problem solving."

Other than being client-centered, the centers do not take any one approach to counseling. Approaches are as varied as the counselors who work at gay services. Those most often mentioned were gestalt, transactional analysis, feminist and radical counseling. All of these are compatible with a non-judgmental stance toward homosexuality.[13]

Evidence leads us to the conclusion that far from being an abnormal peculiarity of our culture, lesbian/gay behavior crosscuts species, cultures, time and space. Cross-species and cross- cultural study of homosexuality has presented us with some broad-based patterns:

1. Homosexuality—both male and female—occurs throughout the nonhuman and human primate order. In the Ford and Beach cross-cultural sample of 76 societies, in 64% (49) of them "homosexual activities of one sort or another are considered normal and socially acceptable for certain members of the community.''[14] Ford and Beach report lesbianism in 17 of the societies in their sample, and Susan Cavin reports on lesbianism in 30 cultures.[15] She found that lesbianism occurs in all major world areas, although from more to less prevalent in the sub-sample of 30 societies: North America (33%), Africa (20%), Insular Pacific (17%), Circum-Mediterranean (13%), South America (10%), and East Eurasia (7%).[16] She found that: ''lesbianism does not appear to be peculiar to any one economy, family or household type, marriage form, stratification [class] system or marital residence.''[17]

Evelyn Blackwood examined the influence of gender and social stratification (class) on lesbian behavior. She pointed out that lesbian behavior occurs within the female gender system and is both ''formal''—''part of a network or social structure extending beyond the pair or immediate love relationship''—and ''informal''—''relations among women which do not extend beyond the immediate social context.''[18] Blackwood cited many specific examples of formal and informal lesbian relations in different cultures. She found that women are more likely to have both formal and informal relations in societies where women have the most control over their activities and status. In class societies women often lack power and either have informal relations or go outside of the dominant culture and organize themselves. Examples are Chinese sisterhoods and American feminist institutions.[19]

2.   **Anthropologists have traditionally ignored study of homosexuality.** Obtaining information on lesbians and male gays in non-Western culture has been an area of neglected research. It is difficult to probe into intimate areas of life in unknown cultures. Language differences provide another barrier. To these reasons can be added the general shrinking from and antipathy toward both studying and reporting data on the

16

existence and nature of lesbian and gay male relations.[20] Anthropologists have been known to collect but not publish data on the subject, and graduate students "may still be reluctant to study homosexuality as a dissertation topic because of the problems it often brings with members of their graduate committees and because they fear it may limit their future employability."[21]

3. Cross-cultural research on lesbianism has been neglected. The paucity of information on lesbians may additionally be due to the neglect of women. Evelyn Blackwood explains a specific factor of neglect: Women were studied in their "normative female role" and in "activities that reflected the western ideology of womanhood as supportive and nurturing of male concerns. Ethnographers focused on the role of women in domestic activities such as gathering, weaving, childbearing, and preparing food for their families, often to the exclusion of women's activities outside the domestic sphere."[22] Blackwood pointed out the problem of selective perception on the part of researchers looking for stereotypic, western-appearing instances of lesbianism—if it didn't look like it did back home or didn't occur in the same kind of circumstances—it was easily overlooked.[23] Then there was the difficulty faced in obtaining information on women by the early, mostly male anthropologists and other observers.

4. Homosexuality seems to be a minority sexual preference. Dr. George Murdock pointed out there is: a biological fact of bisexuality and universal value set on reproduction. In consequence thereof, nearly all societies seek to confine marriage and sex relations to persons of complementary sex.[24]

Homosexuality may occur at specific times chronologically and socially in the life span, such as relations between pubertal boys and older men during puberty initiation rites. Among the Keraki of southern New Guinea, boys are initiated into homosexuality at puberty, being in a passive role for a year and then taking the active role of the adult men.

5. **Homosexuality may conform to particular culturally influenced forms of expression.** For instance, the Keraki of southern New Guinea practice moiety exogamy. Moiety means half and exogamy means marriage outside of. According to this principle of social organization society is divided into two moieties. Members of the same moiety cannot have socially approved sexual and marital relationships. These relationships are supposed to occur between members of opposite moieties.

6. **Homosexuality is more likely to be expressed in cultural situations in which it is not strictly prohibited, seems to arise naturally where not prohibited, and is constrained but not necessarily nonexistent where prohibited.** The figures for homosexuality necessarily are much lower than its actual incidence. Factors have been cultural condemnation by either the people in the culture or by Western investigators, who are known to be condemnatory. The people would therefore tend to hide the existence of homosexual practices from these investigators. Some cultures institutionalize homosexual roles as accepted aspects of society. An example is the berdache institution among the North American Plains Indians, for instance the Mohave. A man may cross-dress and adopt women's economic tasks and sexual role in relation to other men, and marry and settle down with another man. A woman may cross-dress, adopt the male sex role and sex relations, marry and set up a household with other women. The other men and women with whom the cross-role person relates are considered entirely normally adjusted within their sex roles and without onus. In some cultures, for example the Chuckchee of Siberia, the male cross-dresser is also a highly

respected and powerful shaman. Cultures which punish homosexuality may have reduced incidence of it. Children among the Cuna Indians (San Blas Islanders off the eastern coast of Panama), Trukese (Micronesian Islanders), and Sanpoil (North American Indians) are punished severely for actions or tendencies toward homosexuality. Ford and Beach write: ''Among all the societies in which adult homosexual activities are said to be very rare, definite and specific social pressure is directed against such behavior.''[25]

One culture which rates more antipathetic than sympathetic to homosexuality on the scale of cultural response, is our own Judeo-Christian culture. This culture has predominantly been responsible for shaping attitudes toward homosexuality in Western societies. At the time of its genesis and codification of Jewish religious writings—which deal with the range of aspects of religious, social and medical life—the Jewish people were a relatively small, tribal society seeking to multiply in numbers. Homosexuality must have represented an imagined threat to population growth. The attitude against homosexuality spread out geographically and to cultures in other times. These cultures have often been large and not in need of sexual regulation for the sake of reproducing members as quickly as possible. In fact, overpopulation has been the overriding concern. But old traditions die hard and the anti-homosexual philosophy became part of both sacred and secular law and culture. It became institutionalized in the various sectors and institutions of society, noteworthy being upheld by religion, law, medicine, and social mores.

The sacred and secular spheres were once a unified whole, as they largely are in non-Western cultures today. As secular thought proceeded to develop, it went through a process of becoming detached from the sacred realm. At first secular thought mimicked religious thought in its anti-homosexual bias.

19

As scientific study developed and researchers turned their attention to the subject of homosexuality, information was brought to light which supported new perspectives on the subject. For example, Evelyn Hooker compared matched groups of heterosexual and homosexual men and found no significant differences in psychological adjustment.[26] The strength of this information began to be used and have an impact on long-held views. Another force for change came to the fore as homosexuals themselves challenged established views with the force of their very being and justification for their right to be, to love, and to have equal rights and respect as citizens of democratic society.

In turn, secular thought has come to influence the sacred sphere. Those religious persons who espouse the dignity of the human being, democratic principles for organizing society, rationality and factuality have opened themselves and their interpretation of sacred views on homosexuality to question and reconsideration, and some of them have chosen if to err, to err on the side of human reason, ideals and humanitarianism rather than on the side of religious dogmatism. They have separated out the questions of belief in the divine from questions of humanly-conceived law, morality, and practice. One might say that they have followed the "ruach ha din," Hebrew for the "spirit of the law," rather than necessarily the letter of the law. They see God in the spirit, human fallibility in the letter, in its interpretation and application. Others question that the religious text has ever been condemnatory of same-sex relations.

The two approaches to morality are the right-wing dogmatist interpretation of the Bible as condemning homosexuality, and the people who think, look around, and decide for themselves. Some weight has shifted away from the more dogmatic to more reasoned approach to homosexuality only in recent decades, perhaps only beginning in the late 1950s in the United States with empirical research studies into the nature of homosexuality. It definitely gained momentum in the 1960s and grew in the 1970s. The factors which contributed to the crescendo of change included: democratic administrations, the anti-war movement, and especially, the civil and human rights movement of blacks and women. These movements were followed by a noticeable upsurge in the gay movement. In the 1980s the United States has shifted politically to the right again. The right-wing, church fundamentalist—as distinguished from the liberal faction of Christian churches—has led to an onslaught of anti-homosexual religious, legal, and medical attacks. Anita Bryant[27] even has counseling centers to cure homosexuals.

This book deals with the question of the development in the medical/mental health sphere that has occurred in the recent period of struggle and change to a more reasoned approach to homosexuality by chronicling the specific development of lesbian/gay mental health institutions.

The gay counseling service is the lesbian/gay subculture institution which specifically deals with the human suffering resulting from misconceptions, fear, and hostility toward gays. Many of the clients are helped to deal with the hostility, rejection, isolation, denial and nonrecognition with which they live—and with the fear, depression, low self-esteem, anger and emotional turmoil engendered. They come to deal with emerging feelings of a stigmatized identity, loss of family and friends, loss of the feeling of being part of a supportive religion, the difficulties of forming new significant relationships, ways of thinking, and community. Some clients come to deal with genuinely serious psychiatric problems, just as their heterosexual counterparts do at non-gay agencies.

Clients vary in the types of problems presented. At the time of the administration of our national questionnaire[28] in 1979, sexual orientation issues and minor emotional problems were much more frequent than were serious emotional problems.[29] An increase in severity of emotional problems may have occurred since that time due to government prioritization for centers[30] (at least the Seattle Counseling Service) to serve the more seriously disturbed clients.

Another factor which may be involved in the changing pattern of client problems is the change in the status of sexual minorities in society, that is the liberalizing trend in the 1960s and 1970s: more sexual minorities coming out, the gay and feminist movements, and a better educated public. This trend may have made it easier on sexual minority persons to "come out," gain a sense of themselves and a positive relation to both gay subculture and the larger culture. It is reasonable to think that these changes would have resulted in reduced problems of sexual identity and related adjustments for sexual minorities. Problems of mental/emotional disturbance in general and problems of everyday life seemed to gain importance as time went on. However, with the increase in right-wing, anti-gay fanaticism in the 1980s, depression has soared and problems of sexual identity are also increasing.

A greater proportion of clients were in the twenties to early thirties in age, gay, and poor. A small percentage of clients were transsexual and transvestite.[31]

The staff have a great deal to do with shaping the character and style of the Service. This data comes from SCS but the author has every reason to believe that it is typical.

Furthermore, since this is the first published data (as far as the author knows) on the subject, the author welcomes confirmation or refutation of this assumption. The most outstanding variables in staff characteristics have been sex, sexual orientation, political style, lifestyle, and professional/nonprofessional background.

Staff members have been female, male, transgenderal, of various class, race, sexual orientation, age backgrounds, professional or paraprofessional (after in-service training). Staff have been fewer women than men,[32] Caucasian, in the 20s to 40s age range, and a fairly even division between professional and paraprofessional.

A distinction can be made between core and peripheral staff members, core staff being more influential in shaping the agency. The peripherally involved staff members were less likely to earn their livelihood within the gay subculture and more likely to be identified with or similar to others in the larger culture. The core, paid staff were usually former volunteers who worked into their jobs through doing a lot of work and gaining the trust and respect of co-workers.

Although the number of staff members and the turnover rate varies over time, there are usually from twenty-five to fifty staff members. Most of these are volunteers who spend a minimum number of hours per week. Some work intensively for awhile then take a break and resume. Staff usually come to gay counseling services through word of mouth; friends who are staff or clients; advertising, including newspaper ads, public service announcements on radio and television, and leaflets. People who are part of the gay and sexual minority community usually know that these services exist. Others come through school to do fieldwork for credit or as work-study students. A few have come through the probation and parole system—they are required to do community service work and have been assigned to telephone or maintenance work. In some instances, former clients have "gotten it together" and become staff members.

In-service training was provided to every staff counselor, whether they be telephone, in-person or group workers. This might have begun with an intensive day or weekend, followed up by monthly educationals. A new, inexperienced staff member normally starts off doing telephone counseling, and later may or may not become an in-person counselor. Staff members who have professional backgrounds in counseling may quickly become in-person counselors or offer groups.

The motives for staff coming to work at SCS are varied. According to the 1974 staff survey, the most common reason was to serve the gay and sexual minority community. Other common reasons were to help others and to learn. Still others mentioned making up for societal injustice imposed on gay people and politicizing the community. The following reasons were cited in the staff survey of 1977: becoming involved in the gay community, gaining or expanding personal support group, and meeting people. Some came to SCS because they were new in town and had heard about it, and some came for personal growth. A small number came for specialized interests, such as student work programs, the gender program, sexism issues, and political involvement.

All in all, the primary aims of staff in working at SCS have revolved around personal growth, social contact, and a desire to contribute to the gay community. Pertinent to the former reason is the remark made by one of the directors that SCS is really a personal growth center. SCS often has a tremendous impact on staff persons. They may come to SCS with either vague or well-formulated reasons and leave very different people. During the politically oriented periods of SCS history more came for reasons of political commitment or became politicized, committed members of the community. During the more professionally oriented periods, more staff chose or furthered a counseling career through working at SCS.

Staff persons benefit from working in these agencies. In dealing with people at very close range, one gains ideas and tools useful in one's own life, and there is always someone around to talk with. Counselors counsel each other as well as clients. Since personnel are exposed to and can become involved in practically any aspect of agency work—SCS being much more accessible than larger, "establishment" agencies—the opportunity exists for the development of a broad range of knowledge, skills and experiences. Finally, it places one in close, continuing contact with what is going on in the gay and sexual minority community.

SCS staff are proud of the services they provide. The staff survey of 1974 shows that almost all staff wanted SCS to continue indefinitely. Several of these respondents felt that it would be possible to discontinue SCS when and if the larger society no longer discriminated against sexual minorities. No consensus existed among respondents on the question of SCS' relations with the established mental health system. Some did not answer, claiming they did not know enough to do so. Others responded with the following points of view:

SCS is too far from the gay community.

SCS is too close to the gay community.

SCS is too close to the mental health establishment.

SCS should be close to both the gay community and the mental health establishment.

SCS is not too close to either, but there are always dangers in the wings.

SCS should be more political and not accept public funds.

SCS should guard against becoming a conventional agency.

SCS should do more outreach to women, third world people, less aware gays, and the gay community.

The staff survey of 1977[33] indicated some positive responses to SCS relations with the gay community and negative responses toward the established, mental health system. Specific responses included one concerned about getting "out of touch" with the gay community, and three mentioned being "wary" of the established mental health system.

One might ask whether staff or clients get more out of their experience with SCS. Like in other self-help groups, being a staff person may simply be a greater commitment than being a client.

Seattle Counseling Service provides mental health and social services to sexual minorities. It also provides education about sexual minorities to professionals and non-professionals in the fields of social service, and to the public.

The following forms of counseling delivery are provided: telephone counseling, drop-in counseling, and in-person counseling by appointment. Counseling is on an individual or couple/family basis. Therapy groups are also offered.

Telephone counseling is usually the first form of contact the client makes. This may entail: a request for information about available services or how to set up an appointment for in person counseling, or referral. The call may also be for immediate telephone counseling. Many clients prefer the telephone's anonymity to discuss private areas of their sexuality and lives, or they may fear talking to someone in person. For some clients, this contact may be the first or only time they have discussed their sexuality or feelings with another person. Some clients drop in casually to talk or simply to be on the premises for support. Emergency drop-ins are dealt with by whoever is available at the time. Non-emergency drop-ins are usually given an appointment for a future date or put on the waiting list.

In-person counseling is the main form of service. After the initial interview, the client is assigned to a regular counselor. The client may request a counselor with specified characteristics. Lesbians often request a lesbian or other woman counselor, and heterosexual men seem to prefer women counselors. If the counselor and client do not interact well, either may request that another counselor be provided. The counselor and client usually meet once a week for an hour-long session, although more intensive meetings may be required initially or for clients who are more severely disturbed or in crisis. Less frequent meetings are also made as needed and as therapy tapers off. The length of in-person therapy varies from one session to a period of years. Most clients fall in a range of between two and eight sessions.

Groups range from open rap groups to closed, therapy groups focused on particular issues and concerns. Rap groups typically have been for women, men, transgenderals, and transvestites. Other such groups have been bisexual, older men, and gay youth. Still other groups focus on an issue or technique and have included alcoholism, assertiveness training, self-hypnosis, and married gays.

Groups are often advisable for sexual minorities who have had little or no contact with others like themselves. The group functions to "socialize" members. They typically provide a supportive atmosphere for knowledge and skill sharing about how to cope with various life problems. Groups are an important counter to the real and felt isolation which sexual minorities face in the larger social cultural milieu.

Clients may start off with one form of service and change to another. A fairly common progression is from telephone to in-person counseling and finally to a group. As the telephone caller becomes emboldened in seeking help, they may enter in-person counseling. For more seriously disturbed clients, in-person counseling is the most advisable form. After significant progress has been made, in-person clients may be referred to a group, where they can listen to, receive input from, and contribute input to others with similar concerns.

Special programs have existed at SCS for women and transgenderals, who are apt to be neglected and require special sensitivity and specialized programs. Female clients were fewer in number than male clients at SCS and have been encouraged through a special women's program. The numbers of women and especially lesbian clients seem to vary with the number, roles and power of female staff members in relation to male staff members, and with the image and reputation of the Service at a given time as being a good place for women. The fact that specialized women's and lesbian services have sprung up around the country as treatment alternative attests to the demand for these specialized services.

The gender identity program at SCS was the only one in the Northwest United States until the recent establishment of the Ingersoll Gender Center in Seattle. Few gender programs existed in the country when the SCS program arose out of a need for services to this population. Once the program was established, the number of clients requesting services increased. A few transgenderal staff persons in particular have been largely responsible for the success of the program. One was instrumental in starting the program and another for its later development. A gender clinic and sex change operation program once existed at the University of Washington. The SCS program acted in concert with this program in handling candidate screening and counseling for sex reassignment. SCS also cooperated for awhile with an alternative community health clinic which dispensed hormones. While SCS continues to do counseling and groups for gender clients, clients get hormones from local, private doctors, and must go to other cities for operations. There is a dearth of all kinds of resources for this population.

Other programs included an early alcoholics (AA) group, a venereal disease clinic in 1972, and paramedic training. Alcoholism among gays is high and a gay alcohol and drug abuse treatment center later answered the need for such a program in Seattle: The Chemical Dependency Program (CDP) is another stable institution in Seattle's gay community. SCS clients with alcohol and drug problems were referred to CDP or cooperative counseling was done.

The frequency of venereal disease is also high in the gay male population and an SCS staff member set up a VD clinic.[34] Limited by the requirement that body penetration in drawing blood samples be done by licensed medical practitioners and by the high degree of precision necessary in dealing with medical samples, the clinic eventually closed. The staff member negotiated an agreement with the Public Health Service whereby the anonymity of clients was protected. This allowed gay clients and referrals to go to the Public Health Service.

A paramedic training program at the University included information on sexual minorities. The unit was given by someone associated both with the University and SCS, and SCS staff persons were paid to conduct gay bar tours for trainees.

In the current period clients may be referred to other sources: the Chemical Dependency Program (alcohol/drug abuse), Seattle Institute for Sex Therapy, Education, and Research (sex therapy); a lawyer, medical or psychiatric doctor; resources in the sexual minority community, such as gay bars, recreational or social activities and groups, religious or political groups. A client may be referred for help in finding housing, employment, food or public assistance. In rare instances a client will be referred for hospitalization. Resource files and directories are kept by subject and geographic area. Education is another aspect of the program. In-house education has included training programs largely for but not always confined to staff members. This has included lecture, discussion and practice in counseling theory and techniques, and particular topics such as crisis intervention, suicide, drug and alcohol abuse, schizophrenia, VD, and transgenderalism. Educational workshops have been offered on female and male sexuality and the legal system. Large-scale symposia were given for mental health and social service providers (in 1972, 1973), and women and mental health (one of the earliest in the country, in 1975). These symposia were major weekend events with one to two-hundred participants each.

Another aspect of the educational program is speaking engagements to a large number and variety of audiences. These have included: junior and senior high school, college and university, graduate and medical classes, religious and church groups, mental health and social service agencies, hospitals and governmental departments.

Educational engagements with other agencies often function as group consultations. The idea is to help social service personnel do better work with sexual minority persons. Sometimes one-to-one consultation is done with a nonsexual minority therapist or provider working with a sexual minority client who needs additional knowledge, resources or guidance. The consultation may be a one-time contact or ongoing. Consultation may lead to a referral from the non-gay agency to SCS or to another gay agency or resource. Finally, SCS provides advocacy services for clients. This may involve contact with community agencies, hospitals, government, or police department. Sexual minorities are sometime harassed, abused, and treated with hostility by police. One SCS staff member in particular worked in various ways with the police on sexual minority issues. The goal was to gain adequate police protection and to improve police treatment toward sexual minorities.

At one time the police harassed SCS itself, frequently driving by the front and back alley sides of the building, taking license plate numbers, and shining bright lights into the windows. A client almost committed suicide as a result. These practices ceased after a complaint was lodged with the Police Department.

The aforementioned staff person organized a third-party reporting system whereby victims reported rape and assault incidents to SCS. SCS then reported them to the police while maintaining client confidentiality. This Sexual Assault Program was begun in coordination with the Gay Community Center and later became an exclusive program of SCS. There was also cooperative work with Rape Relief and its Sexual Assault Program at a local hospital.

Advocacy has also been done in the legal arena. Jail outreach and visitation programs for sexual minorities in prison were carried out. Sexual minority prisoners often faced dangerous and life-threatening situations due to their sexual minority status.[35]

Sexual minority clients may be accompanied by SCS counselors through the medical and social services systems in order to ensure non-biased, positive treatment of their clients.

---

[1] Originally called Seattle Counseling Service for Homosexuals and later called Seattle Counseling Service for Sexual Minorities, the agency will often be referred to as Seattle Counseling Service, the Service, or SCS.

[2] The survey was administered between 1977 and 1979. There was an N of 70: 13 women, 50 men, 5 transgenderals, 53 homosexuals, and 8 bisexuals. See Appendix D for a copy of the questionnaire. The non-gay counseling services included community mental health centers and private practitioners, representing a variety of counseling options which existed in the Seattle area at the time.

[3] It should not be assumed that marriage means straight; some gays marry. According to Alan Bell and Martin Weinberg, several studies have found that 20% of gays have been married at least once.

[4] Excluded by the term "sexual minorities" are specific sexual practices or categories based on this, such as child molesters, rapists, fetishists, nudists, etc. The term "sexual minorities" was used in the name of SCS to include non-gays, and historically, practical decisions and usage has helped to define who users of SCS are.

[5] Ira Pauley, Adult Manifestations of Male Transsexualism and Sex Reassignment (Baltimore: Johns Hopkins Press, 1969), 60

[6] Another factor is the fact that males are more likely to have the money for the medical expenses.

[7] Alfred Kinsey, Wardell Pomeroy, Clyde Martin and Paul Gebhard, Sexual Behavior in the Human Female (Philadelphia: W. D. Saunders, 1953)

[8] Drs. Pepper Schwartz and Phillip Blumstein are a widely-respected team of sociologists at the University of Washington. They specialize in the study of family and sexual behavior. They authored a book entitled, American Couples: Money, Work, Sex published in 1983. The book is a study of lesbian and gay male couples.

[9] Pepper Schwartz and Phillip Blumstein, "Lesbianism and Bisexuality," Sexual Deviance and Sexual Deviates (New York: William Morrow and Co., 1974)

[10] Phyllis Vine, Families in Pain, Children, Siblings, Spouses and Parents of the Mentally Ill Speak Out (New York: Pantheon Books, 1982)

[11] Ibid., 227

[12] Arthur Lazere, "On the Job, Gay Doctors," Part 3, Seattle Gay News, Section 3 (June 27, 1985), 49

[13] These counseling techniques applied to the mid-1970s. Approaches now include the full range of conventional and alternative therapies, including transpersonal and creative arts. The tendency is toward cognitive and humanistic approaches. This information is based on a personal interview with the current director of SCS about counseling approaches there.

[14] Clellan Ford and Frank Beach, Patterns of Sexual Behavior (New York: Ace Books, Inc., 1951),137

[15] Susan Cavin, Lesbian Origins (San Francisco: Ism Press, 1985), 122-23 Cavin used Murdock's (1957) world ethnographic sample of 565 societies. Out of 64 societies originally in her sample, she excluded 34 societies for several reasons related to their questionable reliability and the useability of the data.

[16] Ibid., 123

[17] Ibid., 126

[18] Evelyn Blackwood, The Many Faces of Homosexuality, Anthropological Approaches to Homosexual Behavior (New York: Harrington Park Press, 1986), 10

[19] Ibid., 10-15

[20] Neglect in studying homosexuality in nonhuman species was historically true as well.

[21] Ibid., xii

33

[22] Ibid.,8

[23] Ibid., 9

[24] George Peter Murdock, Social Structure (New York: The Macmillan Company 1949), 317

[25] Clellan Ford and Frank Beach, Patterns of Sexual Behavior (New York: Ace Books, Inc., 1951) 136

[26] Evelyn Hooker, "The Adjustment of the Male Overt Homosexual," Journal of Projective Techniques, (1957), 18-31

[27] Anita Bryant, movie star, Sunkist orange maid, and popular homophobe, raised anti-gay attacks to new heights in Dade County, Florida in the late 1970s.

[28] The questionnaire is in Appendix D. The questionnaire was done by Joan de Foreest of the Eromin Center in Philadelphia.

[29] See Table C-8 in Appendix C.
In 1985, over 50% of the clients were coming to SCS for problems of depression (28%), sexual orientation (12%), self esteem/self-concept (11%), and sexual orientation (30%).

[30] Government prioritization of services to the seriously disturbed affected SCS and other agencies in the government funded system.

[31] The sample for studies done was weighted by the client characteristics, for example more men than women. However, the purpose for conducting our studies was not to find how to do therapy with particular types of clients. We were looking at the development of a gay institution and its relation to the larger mental health system. Because of the politics of the period, clients were likely to be poor and in their 20s and 30s. It was less likely that professional women in their 40s would be representative in the sample, for instance—especially when the Counseling Service was in its early years. SCS serviced the largest percentage of transgenderals and transvestites. Please refer to Tables 1 and 2 in Appendix C.

[32] There have been proportionately more women than men staff members in the fourth period but this varies.

[33] The author designed the 1974 and 1977 staff surveys.

[34] New Acquired Immune Deficiency Syndrome (AIDS) programs are discussed in chapter 8 with an update on SCS.

[35] Sexual minority prisoners are often sexually and physically assaulted by other prisoners.

CHAPTER 2

"We'll care for
our own —
nobody else
cares for us."

— Author

ESTABLISHED MENTAL HEALTH INSTITUTIONS

ftentimes in the literature the concepts of culture and subculture are not clearly differentiated or are used interchangeably. Dr. James Spradley referred to urban nomads as a "subculture" and a "culture."[1]

An American subculture is "a pattern of living which is distinct from any other Americans and Westerners."[2] Subculture members also have some patterns which they share with members of the larger culture.

The concept of "subculture" had been around a long time and was applied to other groups—and not only to refer to ethnic or racial minorities, which seemed more nearly to fit anthropological tradition of studying non-western peoples—but to the subcultures of urban nomads and streetwalkers. Moreover, there was the famous "culture of poverty" debate launched by Oscar Lewis about whether poor people could be said to have a definable, poverty-based culture. Although in the ensuing argument, the weight went against the notion, along with allegations of racism, it got serious attention for years.

37

To speak of a "subculture" is to recognize the existence of intracultural diversity within the larger culture. A subculture is a unit with shared norms and behavior patterns which differ from those of other subunits and from the larger culture of which it is a part. The anthropological and sociological disciplines define the concept with more or less emphasis on cultural or on social structural components, respectively. More holistic theorists such as Milton Gordon argue for a dynamic relationship between culture and social structure, with ever-changing societal norms and values determining social groupings and social relationships, and the action of individuals within the culture resulting in modification of the culture.

An "institution" is here considered to be a relatively established, commonly occurring structure that is more highly developed and more primary to a subculture than is an "organization" or an "association."

British anthropologists Bronislaw Malinowski (1944) and A. R. Radcliffe-Brown (1935) insightfully formulated the fundamental notion that cultural phenomena arise out of human or social "needs." At a given point in time, cultural phenomena may or may not be adequate to meet these needs, the latter situation being what Walter Goldschmidt terms "inadequate institutionalization."

When needs of members of a subculture are not being met by existing institutions within the larger society, the subculture is compelled to form its own organizations, institutions, and communities. A continuum of social/cultural structures emerge within the subculture to meet the human and distinctively subcultural needs of its members. For example, gay bars are central gay institutions, and, as several authors have pointed out, the starting point for the development of a set of gay institutions.

A similar process occurred at the cultural level in the formation of community mental health centers. The need for increased attention to mental health problems had become obvious with World War II. Additionally, the State hospitals were being deinstitutionalized and patients returned to their communities. A mental health movement formed and with organizing, led to the community mental health centers.

The development of community mental health care centers and the mental health movement, innovative as they were at one time, became the institutionalized and established system to which gay, ethnic and women's services provided an alternative. Whereas community mental health centers are institutions of the larger culture, gay, ethnic and women's services are institutions of their respective subcultures.

Parallel processes can be seen in the historically concurrent examples of gay, racial minority and women's alternative social, mental and medical health care services, which developed out of the gay, racial minority and women's movements and are associated with their respective subcultures.

Social movements develop out of human needs, dissatisfaction with the way things are, and aspiration for change. Movements develop organizations to implement various goals and functions of the movement, with differentiation and specialization of organizational types occurring as necessary. Max Weber and Roberto Michels have asserted that as organizations develop they tend to become increasingly institutionalized and bureaucratic in character.

The gay counseling services were not based on the medical model. Not all counseling at these services is for mental illness, though federal regulations set up and defined mental health programs to serve the mentally ill. Many of the users of the services are not mentally ill as defined in a medical model.

Who has the power to decide questions about who is sick and who is well and the nature of mental health system and services? The community mental health movement raised the issue of whether the community of people were to take control from mental health professionals.[3] Philip Darley wrote an article entitled, "Who Shall Hold the Conch," referring to the conch seashell and the power involved in having it in certain Pacific cultures. He illustrated that an important reason why this is a positive step is the need for mental patients to control their own program. Otherwise they succumb to the belief common among mentally ill and poor—that their life is doomed and societal prejudice toward them is justified.

Empowerment is a process in which these persons "may unlearn what is true in their thinking, may learn the reality of their situation, and may acquire as much control of their life as is available to them."[4] Now this applies to many populations. For example, current cognitive therapies for depression involve relearning.

Clifford Beers began the "Mental Hygiene Movement" earlier in the twentieth century; and mental health policy as it is today developed after World War II.[5] [6] Beers was a former mental patient who "exposed the dehumanizing aspects of mental patient care, out of which emerged a new, humanistic ideology which stimulated some improvement in hospital conditions and public concern for the mentally ill." However, the custodial character of hospital life continued.

A general awareness of the wide prevalence of mental disturbance grew. One out of eight inductees was disqualified from service due to mental illness and 43% of discharges were psychiatric cases.[7]

Congress passed the Mental Health Act in 1946, which created the National Institute of Mental Health in 1949. Monetary investment and mental health professionals grew by leaps and bounds. In 1955 the Mental Health Study Act established the Joint Commission on Mental Illness and Health for a nationwide study of mental health problems. The report of the Commission appeared in 1961 and contained a criticism of state hospitals. This report is said to have heralded community mental health, the application of public health principles to the mental health area, with preventive and environmental emphases. John F. Kennedy proposed that a national program in mental health and retardation be established, resulting in the Community Health Centers Act of 1963 (Public Law 88-164).

This law established that community mental health centers would be located throughout the country. The intent of the community mental health model is that power and decision-making be done by the community concerned, that the conch shells be widely distributed. It was also connected to deinstitutionalization of mental health hospitals. The theory was that return of patients to the community would further their recovery and reintegration. At that time most mental health patients had to stay in hospitals located over 150 miles from home. This made it difficult for relatives and friends to visit them.

In Asylums Erving Goffman wrote convincingly of the "total institution" characteristic of hospitals and prisons, which warehouse human beings and divest them of their identity as individuals and as members of a community. However, the comprehensive community mental health center system has structural problems with regard to who shall hold the conch. The system exists at federal, state and local levels, and some sectors of the population are disinherited at all levels. Money and power come down the system and government imposition can be heavy indeed.

Community mental health centers grew out of a melee of forces: increased awareness of mental health problems and needs, dissatisfaction with the state hospital system, and the growth of the "mental health movement."

The mental health movement as embodied in the comprehensive community mental health center was conceived as meeting all patients' needs regardless of station in life, immediately and with continuity of care. Specific features were: comprehensive services, decentralization to the local level, keeping patients in the community, involvement of the community in mental health care planning and decision-making, and involvement of the practitioner in the community.

The issue of particular relevance to us here is what community is to have controlling power over the nature of mental health services. Specifically, the community mental health centers were inadequate with regard to minorities. As disinherited members of society, sexual and other minorities are unlikely to be "the community" which wields power over the community mental health centers.

In taking power, minorities defied the concept of integrated services, which had been espoused for the community mental health care system. Minorities and women created separate services designed to meet the specialized needs of their own communities.

Medical and mental health services are different. Yet this parallel can be drawn: separate services are a widespread trend. It occurs notably in the free or neighborhood health clinic of the 1960s, which itself was similar to an earlier community health center movement during the 1920s and 1930s.[8] Both were spawned to meet the needs of the urban poor. In the earlier instance, the poor were largely immigrants and in the later instance, largely ethnic/racial minorities. Dr. Sue-Ellen Jacobs described the development, rationale, accomplishments and sociopolitical context of a Free Neighborhood Health Center in a black community in Twin Cities, Illinois. The Black

42

Panther Party developed health care programs in a 'crusade' to shift medical power to the people.''[9]

The free clinics movement has been concerned with broad social issues, placing medicine in an environmental context. It seeks to return health care to the people. The Medical Committee for Human Rights was a grassroots organization first formed in connection with the civil rights movement and was devoted to radical analysis and action.[10]

Dr. Jacobs concluded, along with an observation of a worker in the Free Neighborhood Health Center she studied:

> We have been able to document that many of the problems which low income people face are based on race and class discrimination. The center's efforts are intended to deal with these social problems. In the words of one community worker: ''I'm not sure we're doing the right things here...but one thing I do know for sure, some things in this world have to change, so we're doing it our way, and mostly for our own.[11]

The 1960s was an era of a rising ''peoples' movement.'' The Community Mental Health Centers Act occurred at the same time as the 1964 Civil Rights Act. The popularity of a mental health analysis of pressing social problems mushroomed. Everything and everybody was potentially mentally ill, especially society's more troublesome members.

> The expanson of NIMH [National Institute of Mental Health] mirrored a growing trend in society to extend the definition of mental illness to include a kaleidoscope of disorders from organic and functional disorders to neurotic disorders, alcoholism,

drug addiction, school learning difficulties, juvenile delinquency, employment and marital problems, and even political dissent. By the late sixties some individuals, including a number of psychiatrists, began to see the entire nation as mentally ill and brought into vogue the epithet "the sick society."[12]

The idea arose that the best therapist is the one who has the problem. A variety of self-help groups arose, including Alcoholics Anonymous, groups for ex-mental patients, weight loss, and self-fulfillment. Peer Self-Help Psychotherapy Groups (PSHG) were felt as a threat by establishment psychotherapists and were criticized.[13] But the die was cast: alcoholics, drug addicts, prisoners, poor, blacks, and gays would care for their own. A consciousness now emerged which viewed mental, emotional, economic, social, cultural and political problems as a whole. Larry Dossey wrote: "The struggle for health is a struggle against fragmentation and disunity."[14] It was recognized that who controls therapy, who defines the problem and the solution, makes a significant difference.

Social theorists and radical activists in the 1960s spoke of a sense of alienation from modern, technological society and a need to return to a sense of individual worth and community. Return to the community concept was evidenced in the overall culture and in community mental health care. It was also evidenced subculturally in alternative social services in which people took the conch into their own hands.

For the reader with little familiarity with cause and cure[15] theories of homosexuality, the balance of this chapter will provide an overview useful in putting the entire argument in context.

The culture is basically antipathetic to homosexuality. Therefore, it is not surprising that early theories of causation have as their common denominator an assumption of homosexuality's essential wrongness. Societal fear and prejudice and the almost uniformly hostile social/cultural environment in which gays have found themselves have historically resulted in treating homosexuality as a problem in need of cure.

In The Manufacture of Madness, Thomas Szasz described an historical succession of prevailing attitudes toward homosexuality: homosexuality as sin; homosexuality as crime; homosexuality as sickness, physical or psychological. Actually these models are not historically discrete; all three perspectives exist today to some extent in some sectors of society. The homosexuality as sin attitude is particularly prevalent in the 1980s among right-wing, Christian extremists.

The Judeo-Christian tradition, as historically interpreted by religious authorities in the established churches and synagogues, has viewed homosexuality as a sin against God. The concept of homosexuality as crime—as a "sin" against society, so to speak—is a secularization of the religious notion of homosexuality as sin. Today many people retain both notions simultaneously, associated with deeply-held religious beliefs and unquestioning allegiance to secular law, even when applied to "victimless crimes."

In the nineteenth and early twentieth centuries, the concept of homosexuality as a physical or psychological sickness emerged to compete with still extant theories of homosexuality as sin or crime.

A theory of physical causation was first propounded by Dr. Carl Westphal in 1870. It became well known through Richard von Kraft-Ebing's widely-circulated 1882 work, Psychopathia

Sexualis. This view, shared by others in the late 1800s, was that homosexuality was a congenital, hereditary degenerative state which was, in some cases, impacted by acquired influences. Negative as this formulation was, gays at the time may have preferred the idea that they were born into their homosexuality to the sin and criminal theories still widely prevalent. Viewing gayness as a congenital, degenerative state afforded gays some protection from demands for punishment and cure.

In the years preceding World War II, a psychological approach to causation gained currency, particularly as articulated by Sigmund Freud and his followers. Freud believed that humans are born bisexual, and either do or do not progress through stages of psychosexual development. Homosexuality, then, was not to be considered a sickness in the strict sense, but an arrested state of development. Freud's disciples applied Freud's theories of penis envy, mother fixation and the Electra complex to explain the etiology of lesbianism. They postulated that male homosexuality stemmed from identification with women, mother fixation, and narcissism, that is, choice of oneself as a sexual object. After experiencing a lifetime of difficulty attempting to treat his gay patients with psychoanalytic methods, in his later works Freud stated his belief that a psychoanalytic approach alone is inadequate in this area and needs to be supplemented by biological research. Some present-day Freudians are more Freudian than Freud in their dogmatic adherence to psychoanalytic approach, theory and treatment as the only viable way to illuminate the cause and effect the cure for homosexuality.

The theories reviewed so far are either "armchair" or clinical in nature—that is, someone either thought them up, or based them on one or a small number of patients. Neither approach meets minimal standards of scientific research. The former seeks to discern reality through subjective introspection. The latter makes general assertions regarding an entire population based on a patient population which is unrepresentative of the majority, non-patient population.[16]

Post-Freudian theorists are generally of two schools: those who view homosexuality as a problem for which there must be a cure, and those who view societal homophobia as the problem requiring change.

Some have suspended value judgment and conducted empirical research to illuminate the phenomenon of homosexuality. In 1957 Evelyn Hooker conducted the first non-patient-centered study of male homosexuals and matched heterosexuals. She found no significant differences in psychological adjustment between the homosexual and the heterosexual groups. Many empirical studies of male homosexuality followed: Liddicoat, Schofield, Doidge and Holzman, Change and Block, Cattell and Morony, Miller, Dean and Richardson, Deluca, and Saghir).

While most of the empirical studies found numerous areas of commonality between homosexual and heterosexual subjects, some of the studies found differences which are intriguing—the findings delineated lesbian characteristics, many of them positive in comparison with heterosexual counterparts:

FINDING	RESEARCHER	DATE
independent	Armon	1960
self-sufficient	Hopkins	1969
self-confident	Thompson	1980
goal-directed, less depressed	Siegelman	1972
cautious, cool, reserved	Armon	1960
more inclined to cross-role preference	Saghir	1970
likely to possess defense mechanisms of hostility, fear and guilt from early childhood relations	Armon	1960
more likely to have alcoholic father	Bene	1965
more likely to be alcoholic and suicidal	Saghir	1970
likely to have greater counseling readiness	Rosen	1971

Even a cursory examination of the diverse theorizing and research regarding homosexuality leaves one confounded by the great variation among homosexuals in personality, behavior and background. This welter of information becomes comprehensible only if one concludes that homosexuality is not a disease entity or a state of ill-health, but rather a term labeling the sexual preference of a cross-section of the population.

Some post-Freudian theorists and practitioners consider "cure" impossible, and inappropriate, while others, unfortunately, believe "cure" possible and recommend methods to affect it. Techniques for "cure" have involved jailing, hospitalization, visits to brothels, abstention from masturbation, and avoidance of harmful influences (such as over-close association with persons of the same sex and with perverse individuals). Frontal lobotomy, electric shock, aversion therapy and anti-androgen drugs have been mobilized in the service of molding sexual desire into a morally and psychologically acceptable form or obliterating it entirely. Although research and experience overwhelmingly indicate that psychotherapy is ineffective in changing sexual preference, it is currently the most popular method of "cure." The traditional psychotherapeutic approach ranges from compulsory internment, to a protracted, costly, series of office visits to a mental health practitioner.

As elements of the gay subculture consciously rejected cultural standards regarding sexual deviancy, the need grew for a gay mental health delivery system based on the premise that gays have legitimate mental health needs and that gayness itself is not a sickness. The need grew for mental health practitioners who did not presume sin, crime or illness, nor admonish their gay clients to take a more "normal" place on the bell curve of sexual preference.

The old nature or nurture controversy has been legendary

with regard to homosexuality. Psychological theories and studies have company in biological theories and studies.

People usually distinguish a person's sex according to how they look externally, or their external genitalia. The sexual index, according to which most newborns are assigned their sex membership, is based on external morphology. However, sex can be gauged at the chromosomal, gonadal, hormonal, internal and external morphological, and neural levels biologically, not to mention psychological, social and cultural sex. Furthermore, these different levels for gauging sex may be out of keeping with each other. While most individuals are biologically either all female or all male at each level, this concordance can and does break down at all levels, creating a variety of anomalies or irregularities from normal variation. Thus, somebody who may look like one sex and be assigned to that sex, may be the other sex chromosomally, or gonadally, or hormonally, or some combination of male and female at different of these levels. Individuals who have such a mixture of female and male characteristics are variously designated and classified by medical and popular terms; e.g. hermaphrodite. All taken together are called "intersexes" because they are somewhere between the male and female sexes.

John Money and John Hampson take an environmental point of view. Hampson studied 113 patients with varieties of biological anomalies. He studied 19 cases in which sex chromatin pattern and sex of rearing were contradictory; 30 cases in which gonads and sex of rearing were contradictory; 31 cases in which hormonal sex and sex of rearing were contradictory; 25 cases in which external genitalia and sex of rearing were contradictory.

In almost all cases, the gender role was in keeping with the sex of rearing rather than the biological factors studied. He therefore concluded that gender role and orientation are learned. He also found that gender role can be successfully changed only up until the individual concerned is eighteen months to two years of age, after which there is a much decreased chance of a successful transition.

The environmentalists postulate that humans are sexually neutral at birth and that sexual orientation is developed according to life experiences.

Those who take a biological point of view believe that sexual orientation is established before birth. Research has centered around chromosomal, hormonal, and neural factors.

Many studies have shown that when female animals (guinea pigs, rats) are exposed to testosterone before and shortly after birth, that is, at critical periods of development, female sexual behavior is lacking and male sexual behavior is present; and vice versa, that when male animals are deprived of testosterone before and shortly after birth, male sexual behavior is lacking and female behavior ensues.

The hormone androgen is implicated as crucially important to sexual orientation. A number of investigators[17] have delineated two roles for androgen, at early and later periods of development. At the early period, either prenatally or shortly after birth, varying by species, androgen is involved in the organization and differentiation of the nervous system as male or female. If testosterone is sufficiently present in the brain at the critical period, the animal is organized as male; and if testosterone is not present at the critical period, the animal is organized as female.

Estrogen is also a relevant hormone in relation to sexual orientation. Administration of estrogen early after birth results in a lack of responsiveness to female hormones in adulthood. Administration of estrogen early after birth and administration of testosterone in adulthood results in male sexual behavior on the part of females.

Some researchers have found that homosexuals have an intermediate level in the balance between male and female hormones between their own sex and that of the opposite sex.

Given the differentiating function of testosterone in the brain at a critical period, the question arises as to what part of the brain is involved. Investigators have implicated various areas of the brain, including the hypothalamus and the limbic[18] system and parts thereof, which are connected with the hypothalamus and influence it. A third viewpoint is that the whole brain is implicated with local areas secondarily important.

Many animal studies have shown a genetic or inherited aspect of sex. For the human, Franz Kallman's study showed forty, male homosexual, monozygotic twins with 100% concordance rates. That is, in every case of a man being homosexual, his identical twin was also. This type of research is used to show that the characteristic in question is genetically determined. Many subsequent twins studies to Kallman's have shown both agreement and disagreement with his finding of a genetic basis for homosexuality.

While psychologically and biologically oriented researchers have actively pursued the question of the causation of homosexuality for years, none of the postulated causes has been consistently substantiated. Perhaps this is because researchers have been looking for a single cause when no such thing exists. Of course, once 'the cause'' is supposedly found, this provides justification for finding ''the cure'', and this is a questionable endeavor at best.

Another school of thought takes culture into account. It looks at how the culture defines, calls, or labels who and what is sick.

Cognitive, psychological and medical anthropoligists have shown that cultural conceptions and categories largely define the ''background'' against which health and illness, normality and abnormality are delineated. As one defines the background differently, one's perception of the object portrayed in the picture changes.

In the 1930s, Ruth Benedict broke through the ethnocentric prejudices of her day with her assertion that much behavior, including homosexuality, is culturally relative. That is, consideration of a behavior as normal or abnormal is not uniform cross-culturally, but varies with the culture's definition of the behavior.

Application of subsequently developed social role, social interaction and labeling theories to this issue illuminates the practical importance of cultural definition to the gay individual. Labeling theorists note the power of the label itself: if people concur and respond to the labeling of someone as deviant, they will be treated as deviant and may easily come to view themself as deviant as others continually interpret their actions as sustaining that definition. The deviant status becomes crucial to the interpretation of all the individual's actions, even within spheres of behavior unrelated to the area in which the individual is judged to be deviant.

Social role theorists Earl Rubington and Martin Weinberg found that persons were more quickly labeled deviant by others who were socially distant from them or had a different cultural or class background. From this, it can be inferred that social-cultural minorities are more likely to be labeled as deviant by the majority. John Kitsuse discussed the question of societal reaction to homosexuality specifically and the formation of a definition of it as deviance.

Certainly it is not justifiable to argue for uncritical acceptance of the culture's definition of deviancy as the truth. As noted above, the definition varies cross-culturally. Within a single culture, it varies with time as different influences within a culture predominate. Like much of human behavior, human sexual orientation is complex. We are biological and psychological and social and cultural and spiritual beings.

---

[1] James Spradley, You .Owe Yourself a Drunk, An Ethnography of Urban Nomads (Boston: Little, Brown and Company, 1970), 263

[2] Ibid., 98

[3] From another perspective, the mental health professionals were to give/return control to the people. How you see it is a function of where you're sitting.

[4] Philip Darley, "Who Shall Hold the Conch," Community Mental Health Journal, Vol. 10, No. 2 (1971), 185-91.

[5] David Mechanic, Mental Health and Social Policy (Englewood Cliffs: Prentice-Hall, 1969, 1980), 61 of World War II.15.

[6] This raises the question as to whether mental illness was that generation's safe way out of the war or whether war is crazy-making or whether acting crazy is a sane response to war.

[7] Elizabeth Hartner, personal communication (University of Pittsburgh, 1972)

[8] George Rosen, "The First Neighborhood Health Center Movement, Its Rise and Fall," American Journal of Public Health, Vol. 61 (1971), 1620-37

[9] Sue-Ellen Jacobs, "Doing It Our Way and Mostly For Our Own," Human Organization, Vol. 33, No. 4 (1974), 380-82

[10] Robert Bazell, "Health Radicals: Crusade to Shift Medical Power to the People," Science, Vol. 173 (1971), 506-9

[11] Jacobs, 382

[12] Franklin Chu and Sharland Trotter, The Madness Establishment (New York: Grossman, 1974), 8

[13] Dorothy Tennov, Psychotherapy, The Hazardous Care (New York: Anchor Books, 1976), 200-201

[14] Larry Dossey, Beyond Illness , Discovering the Experience of Health (Boulder, Colorado: New Science Library, 1984), 122

[15] There is no "cause" and no "cure" for homosexuality. Anything reputed to be either of these is false and misleading. Human sexuality is far too complex to be said to have a single cause, and the concept of cure is inappropriate for something that is not a disease condition.

[16] The author's studies based on samples from SCS are biased in that sexual minorities in treatment may not be representative of sexual minorities in general.

[17] Geophrey Harris, "Sex Hormones, Brain Development and Brain Function," Endocrinology, Vol. 75 (1975), 627-48

[18] The limbic system is the phylogenetically (developed through evolution) old mammalian brain. It is connected with the hypothalamus and influences it. The limbic system is concerned with emotions and motivations.

CHAPTER 3

''There will always be a degree of variance in life style for gay people that is better under-stood by an agency which is in tune and touch with the specific culture of its clientele.''

— Client

LESBIAN/GAY SUBCULTURE

Until recent times, the issue of the existence of a gay subculture was not discussed. The semi-hidden nature of gay life prior to the 1970s, and the stigmatization and lack of attention afforded gay life in the straight and academic worlds combined to preclude serious study of the question in academia. When the author began work on the subject of this book in the 1970s, some anthropological colleagues virtually scoffed at the idea that there could be a lesbian/gay subculture. Some debate occurred in the literature as to whether there was such a thing as a gay ''culture,'' though little discussion concerned the concept of subculture.

Yet perhaps less than academically credentialed lesbian and gay authors felt quite free and yes, happy, to discuss gay ''culture,'' although they were often talking about high culture, that is, music, theater, art. One can readily see how the lines were drawn up.

As time has gone on, there is more and more mention of lesbian and gay ''culture'' and ''subculture.'' After all, lesbians and gays have been noticeably around for awhile in our recent memory and they seem to be developing, well, culture, as time goes on.

We have said that a subculture is a distinct pattern within a larger culture, and it is our contention that lesbians and gay men have such a distinct pattern of subculture.

Study and discussion about lesbians and gays was largely about the how they got that way and what to do about them now variety, religious issues, lifestyle issues, such as couples and lesbian/gay parentage, what lesbians and gays are like, or the lesbian/gay institution—the bar. This study fits no stereotype and strikes out on its own to study another lesbian/gay institution—the gay counseling service.

The lesbian/gay subculture has its own rationale, organizations, institutions, traditions and rituals. Viewed within such a context, the phenomenon of gay counseling services becomes clearly comprehensible. Gay counseling services have their roots in the gay movement and the mental health movement, both of which developed about the same time. Their system of cultural meanings derives from their gay subculture. Their interactions are with their respective gay communities and the mental health system of the larger culture. Their organization is more or less traditional.

Some of the controversy regarding application of the term "subculture" to gay life may stem from taking an unrealistically dichotomous, either-or approach to the question of applying the concept of subculture. The question is more accurately one of extent of applicability. As with the concept of "race," there is a continuum of variation in the realities of "gay." Close-ended, dichotomous definitions are arbitrary, masking the empirical reality.

In reviewing the literature we find that as time goes on, more favorable views as to the existence of a lesbian/gay subculture or culture are expressed.

The writings of John Gagnon and William Simon in the early 1970s contend that while there is a homosexual "community" in most large cities, it is, or was, at that time, "an impoverished cultural unit.'' From Gagnon and Simon's perspective, this is not necessarily negative because most gays must participate in the larger society. Participation by gays in the homosexual community results in ''reducing their anxiety and conflicts in the sexual sphere and increasing the quality of their performance in other aspects of social life.''

Joseph Harry and William DeVall take issue with the characterization of the homosexual community as an ''impoverished cultural unit.'' They argued back in 1978 that the hypothesis is a dated one. Gays in rural areas, married heterosexual men, and those participating in the community on a limited and largely sexual basis may have experienced the community as ''impoverished.'' For others, Harry and DeVall note the recent growth in a gay sense of identity, institutions, political culture, and recreational styles. Much growth in the gay subculture has occurred since 1978.

Laud Humphreys (1979) stressed the necessity of examining the actualization and visibility of gay culture in the context of the social/political/cultural realities of the larger culture which have impacted it. He postulated that what one believes one knows about gay subculture must be viewed against a background which clarifies the ''tendency of dominant cultures to suppress, bowdlerize, distort, ban and obliterate the literary and historical records of 'dangerous classes'.''[1]

In his 1980 ethnography of a male homosexual tavern, Kenneth Read wrote of the ''style'' of a male homosexual tavern. He argued that it is only minimally useful to speak of a homosexual ''culture'' because extensive diversity of lifeways overshadows commonality of same gender sexual preference. In developing this argument, he noted: diversity of gay men by ethnic, racial, educational, economic, occupational, religious, and political status; lack of a completely shared language; lack of participation of the majority of gays as activists in a gay movement; and the lack of cooperation between gay men and women. Dr. Read maintained that the majority of homosexuals are "Middle Americans," and that Middle American values "are more important to most of them than open identification by sexual preference."

While Dr. Read's points are well taken, this author thinks that sufficient divergence from the larger culture and similarity between gays merits the recognition of a gay subculture, within which are a variety of what Dr. Read has identified as "styles."

Michael Bronski (1984) conceptualized gay subculture as a reaction to the dominant culture of patriarchal heterosexuality and a shaper of the gay subculture. He also recognized an interaction as gays take effective action to change the larger culture and gay subculture infiltrates it.

Karla Jay (1979) and Sasha Lewis (1979) acknowledge the associated theme of a two-way interaction between gay subculture and the larger heterosexual culture. This is certainly the case with gay counseling services in interaction with the mental health establishment.

Karla Jay traced the development of a "lavender culture." Prior to the Stonewall Riot of 1969 and the advent of the Gay Liberation Movement, Jay believed that because of the central fact of the willing or unwilling integration of gays into the larger culture, gay culture consisted largely of borrowed and/or transformed aspects of mainstream heterosexual culture. Since 1969 emphasis within the gay movement has shifted from a predominant desire for integration into the larger society, toward positive feeling regarding development of an intrinsically gay culture and change of the larger culture.

Many feel that there are significant enough differences between lesbian and gay male culture to differentiate between two distinct subcultures, as well as the subcultures or styles, to use Dr. Read's term. This author agrees that a lesbian subculture can be delineated. For the purposes of studying lesbian/gay counseling services in this book we have emphasized the lesbian/gay subculture.

Both Deborah Wolfe and Sasha Lewis examined the complexity and range of lesbian life. Wolfe distinguished lesbian cultural feminists from lesbian feminist socialists, and contrasts "old gay life" of the 1950s which centered around bars and "homophile self-help organizations" with the newer, activist, lesbian community. She delineated shared assumptions within the activist feminist lesbian community regarding self, classification of people, nature of relationships, cosmology and the world.

Sasha Lewis highlighted the diversity among lesbian women in describing subdivision of lesbian women into a "subculture in hiding" and an "activist" subculture—the former composed primarily of older lesbians self protective of their careers and security who survived the McCarthy era, the latter composed of "out of the closet"[2] women organizing for civil rights. Lewis believed the passage of time and the anti-gay backlash of the late 1970s are promoting increased understanding and cooperation between these groups.

Denyse Lockard distinguished key concepts: "Lesbian population" is defined as "those women who identify themselves as lesbian;"[3] "lesbian community" is defined as "composed of social networks of lesbians;"[4] and "lesbian subculture" is defined as "the shared values and norms of the lesbian subculture...shared among lesbians who are present or former members of a lesbian community."[5] She delineated four features of the lesbian community and gives an ethnographic example of a large southwestern city (unnamed). Lesbian subcultural values are portrayed as "synonymous with feminist values as expressed in the most active and visible segments of the lesbian communities and held to some degree by other participating members...The lesbian subculture provides a women-oriented alternative to the values and concerns of the heterosexual world.''[6]

These definitions and the related material are in keeping with this author's perceptions of the meaning of the terms defined and the lesbian subculture.

The variegated nature of lesbian and gay male life elaborated by the authors reviewed lends richness and depth to what is indeed a very complex tapestry. Such diversity need not preclude referring to this complex picture as a subculture.

This author will use the concept of gay subculture with the following understandings:

1. There is a lesbian/gay departure from the larger culture which is based on sexual orientation.

Much culture surrounds sexual identity. Major cultural institutions—marriage, the family, indeed the entire culture—are permeated with a heterosexual model. There is a generalizing effect whereby sexual identity affects myriad aspects of life and self-definition. Historically the norm in Western cultures has been fundamentally anti-homosexual, with the successive presentation of gayness as sinful, criminal, or sick.

Upon entering the gay subculture one's status changes from one of social stigmatization to one of relative worth. Oftentimes this transition leads to much personal change as the individual experiences both liberation and discomforting disruption. This may involve psychological internalization of norms, removal of feelings of suppression, surfacing of feelings of selfhood, sensed or real loss of friends and family, job, home, and security. Additionally, new problems may arise relating to alienation, loneliness, sexuality, interpersonal relationships, the need to develop new friendships, support systems and resource networks, and the need to generally reorient oneself in lifestyle, beliefs and values. The individual may seek counseling and subcultural affirmation to cope with the culture shock of "coming out" from one culture and coming into a gay sub-culture.

A person might be "out of the closet" or "in the closet" with reference to oneself, sexual partners, the gay subculture, or the culture at large. A person can be said to come out of the closet repeatedly, with one's friends, parents, co-workers, the media, etc. The sense in which these terms have been used has shifted historically from the sense of coming out sexually, that is one's first homosexual experience, to letting others know. There seems to be a progression from letting others know within the gay subculture to letting others know who are outside the gay subculture and not themselves gay.

2. There are varying "lifestyles" within the gay subculture based on both cultural and subcultural lines of diversity.

Gay subculture is not monolithic. Its members derive from the larger culture which is replete with cultural difference associated with sex, race, ethnic group, class, age, religion and creed. Examining gay life, one sees an incompletely melted pot which has been poured from another incompletely melted pot.

Major divisions occur along sex, race and class lines as is true of the larger society. Most visible gay subculture is white. Racial minority people who are sexual minorities carry the multiple burden of racist and anti-gay culture, an anti-gay racial minority subculture and a racist gay subculture. If they are women, they carry the additional burden of sexism.

Inside the gay subculture the lesbian/gay male division is primary. Development of gay male culture has tended toward the sexual arena and public territories as expressed in bars, baths, tearooms, and drag shows. Gay male culture also includes rap and health support groups, clinics, gay media, and men's choirs.

Lesbian culture includes public territories such as lesbian bars. Much of lesbian life has been influenced by the women's movement. There are lesbian and women's centers; consciousness-raising and rap groups; women's dances; music and spirituality festivals; work collectives; non-traditional trade associations; lesbian and women's media, literature, art, music; clinics; rape and battered women centers; and religious alternatives (e.g. goddess worship).

Both lesbian and gay male culture encompass participation in the gay movement. Additionally, lesbian culture includes participation in a specifically lesbian movement.

Class differences divide the gay subculture. Economic disparities affect what individuals can and cannot do from a financial standpoint. Class differences affect lifestyle and the kind of social and political participation within the gay movement to which the individual is drawn.

In addition to the subcultural diversity which is a reflection of larger cultural diversity, there are specifically gay lifestyle variations. These variations can be split into more or fewer categories. An individual may participate in one or more categories simultaneously. Some salient categories are gay activists of both conservative and radical persuasions, the bar crowds, participants in the court and ball scene,[7] and those involved in gay institutions or organizations, for examples religious groups, community centers and counseling services.

3.   Gay persons participate to lesser or greater extents in gay subculture and lifestyles.

At one extreme are gay persons whose sole contact with gay life is a sexual one. At the other extreme are those who almost completely, although never entirely,[8] live their lives inside the subculture. Between these extremes is every variant of participation.

Closeted gays participate less in gay subcultural arenas than those who are out of the closet, and gay activists participate to a greater extent. Degree of participation may change over time as well. Jack Hedblom found that the succeeding stages of lesbian identity development were phantasy, active sexual involvement, and commitment to the lesbian community.

4. Lesbian/Gay subcultural structures are more or less like or unlike larger cultural structures.

While some associations and institutions are to a large degree modeled on similar structures in the larger culture, others do not have an analogue in the larger culture. In the religious realm, for example, Metropolitan Community Church (a gay church widespread in the United States), Dignity (a large, gay Catholic organization), and Integrity (a gay Episcopalian organization) are similar to larger cultural religious organizations. Goddess worship, by contrast, is different from any larger cultural manifestation. We will examine the ways in which gay counseling services are an analogue to mental health services in the larger culture.

5. Historic and geographic or "community" differences influence the immediate character of lesbian/gay subculture.

Although gay people often refer to "the gay community," as discussed above, there is not, in fact, one monolithic gay community. History, location, lifestyle differences, and interaction with the larger community and with other subcultures delineate the character of particular lesbian/gay communities.

When one understands lesbian/gay subculture and the growth of gay counseling services from that subculture, one can understand the pressing need for gay counseling services as a subcultural institution.

One may come to reject cultural standards, but it is difficult if not impossible to completely escape their influence. The evolution of gay movement organizations in the United States undeniably exhibits the hallmarks of the attitudes of the larger society in which the gay subculture is inextricably embedded.

The period prior to the early 1920s can be labeled Pre-Organizational, because little of what can be called gay community existed in the heavy climate of suppression and punishment which encouraged gays to remain closeted and isolated. The first known gay association, The Chicago Society for Human Rights, founded in 1924, was short-lived, disbanding after only one year of existence when its members were jailed for being homosexual.

The Homophile[9] Period of the 1950s and 1960s saw the rise of such organizations as the Mattachine Society, The Daughters of Bilitis, Society for Individual Rights, and ONE. The homophile organizations of this period had an integrative philosophy vis-a-vis the larger culture congruent with the climate of a time which included the McCarthy hearings and predominately adjustment oriented psychological approaches.

The famous 1969 Stonewall Riot in New York City's Greenwich Village marked the beginning of the Gay Liberation Period. Gays increasingly abandoned efforts at gaining acceptance in the larger society, in favor of enunciating the ever more staunchly-held conviction that "gay is good" and that gays must be accorded their full human and political rights.

A major function of the 1950s Homophile Period of the gay movement was counseling.[10] This fit with the Homophile philosophy of homosexual "adjustment" and "integration" into society. These phrases were used for example, in the statement of purpose of the Daughters of Bilitis, the first lesbian organization in the United States.

By the early 1960s a struggle surfaced between homophile factions over how to view homosexuality. The Society for Individual Rights looked to mental health professionals to redefine gay as good. The Mattachine Society split: one faction advocated study by mental health professionals to find out whether gay is good; and the other faction defined gay as good. In 1965 Mattachine took a stand to formally oppose the American Psychiatric Association's classification of homosexuality as an illness. Ultimately this latter view predominated in the Gay Liberation Period of the movement. The call of gay liberationists was not for adjustment to society; the call was for society to change. The problem was redefined—homosexuality was not the problem; societal homophobia (literally, fear of homosexuality) was/is.

The gay movement adopted confrontation tactics to change mental health professional views of homosexuality. In 1970 and 1971 gay activists seized the microphone at the American Psychiatric Association's annual meetings. In 1972 a gay psychiatrist was invited to speak, leading to a resolution to delete homosexuality as an illness. A Nomenclature Task Force was set up, which became the focus of gay activist pressure. In that year the gay liberation organization, the Gay Activists Alliance, zapped[11] the convention of behaviorists in protest of the aversion therapy techniques used for the treatment of homosexuals. Ronald Gold, along with Dr. Charles Silverstein and others on both sides of the fence, spoke on a panel at the 1973 meetings. Gold said: "Your profession of psychiatry dedicated to making sick people well, is the cornerstone of a system of oppression that makes people sick."[12] In December 1973 the Board of Trustees of the American Psychiatric Association accepted a resolution which reclassified homosexuality as an illness. It was now to be called a "sexual orientation disturbance" for those "who are either bothered by, in conflict with, or wish to change their sexual orientation." Gay activists questioned why this category remained. Was it done to protect psychiatry for its long record of harm to gays and to allow that to continue by reason that unhappy gays should be encouraged to get a therapeutic "cure." What about the insight that negative psychiatric categorizing was a major factor contributing to gay unhappiness.

Nevertheless, it had been admitted that self-accepting gays should not be labeled as ill. The following resolution was adopted:

> Whereas homosexuality per se implies no impairment in judgment, stability, reliability, or general social or vocational capabilities, therefore, be it resolved that the APA deplores all public and private discrimination against homosexuals in such areas as employment, housing, public accommodations, and licensing and declares that no burden of proof be placed upon homosexuals greater than that imposed on any other persons. Further, the APA supports and urges the enactment of civil rights legislation singling out homosexual acts by consenting adults in private.

The American Psychological Association at a meeting in January 1975 declared that: "Homosexuality per se implies no impairment in judgment, stability, reliability or general social or vocational capabilities." It was also stated that the Association "deplores" discrimination against gay people and urged gay civil rights legislation and the repeal of anti-gay legislation. The Association of Gay Psychologists, organized in 1973, was largely responsible for this achievement.

Other lesbian/gay professional organization caucuses of nurses, social workers, and public health workers have more recently joined the struggle. They have been actively working "within the system" for positive changes in attitudes and treatment of gays.

There are pros and cons of working from within professional organizations. On the pro side, more change can occur in dialogue with colleagues. On the con side, this may tend to scatter and isolate lesbian/gay professionals from different disciplines; and it may present a more satisfied or apathetic veneer to the outside world.

Despite the fact that professional organizations declassified homosexuality as an illness, many practitioners continued to treat homosexuals as mentally ill. Mental health practitioners continued to collude with legal and religious forces to uphold cultural homophobia and gay persecution.

Disillusioned, hurt and angry with both established psychiatry and so called "community" mental health centers, gay professionals and non-professionals moved to set up their own counseling services, dedicated to helping gays in a positive way and in their own terms.

Lesbian/gay mental health workers are important resources for the mental health field and society. They must stand up and be counted, and they must be empowered by the mental health system to be able to make contributions to their fields. They must be hired by mental health centers and schools and help to hire others.

The gay movement grew out of gays' dissatisfaction with and need to change their stigmatized status to one of equality with other members of society.

Gay organizations developed to implement the goals and functions of the gay movement. Gay social services and counseling services formed to fulfill the specialized function of meeting mental health needs not being met by the established mental health system. Gay counseling services became institutions within the gay subculture, and have become increasingly institutionalized in character.

Gay counseling services are key gay subcultural institutions, which were established to fulfill the unmet need for appropriate, problem-specific mental health/social services free of a bias against homosexuality. The depth of this need is documented by the description of the characteristics of users of counseling services for sexual minorities and their interactions with the established mental health system. Gay counseling services provide services from a subcultural standpoint, and they function as an agent of both personal and cultural change.

Stating that unmet needs within the gay community led to development of gay counseling services is useful in illuminating the cause of this subcultural institution at a broad, conceptual level. It leaves unexamined the mechanism by which something as subjective and internalized as a need becomes manifest as an objective institutional structure.[13]

The process whereby unmet needs in the gay community led to development of gay counseling services can be represented:

Unmet Needs	Unmet Needs
Social Movement	Gay Movement
Movement Organization	Gay Movement Organization
Institution	Gay Counseling Services

This model of institutional development appears to have applicability to other instances and populations. Undoubtedly had the gay movement not occurred, gay counseling services would not have arisen. Gay counseling services developed out of the gay movement, and directly or indirectly out of gay movement oraganizations, to become institutions of gay subculture.

Many alternatives to human services have been spawned by American subcultures, including lesbian/gay, women, and ethnic/racial minorities. These human service institutions provide subculturally sensitive and knowledgeable services to members of their respective subcultures. Sometimes these alternative services are used to the exclusion of establishment services.

The centers[14] view themselves as "alternative"[15] to the traditional or "establishment" mental health system. The centers differ in the extent to which they fit into the established mental health system. Some centers have stayed outside that system financially and otherwise, with some fearing such an association. These wished to avoid dependence, bureaucratization, alienation from their gay communities, and the threat of losing client confidentiality and integrity.

Respondents to the national questionnaire answered the question: "Would you like to be part of the established mental health system and why or why not?" Three answers given were:

No, it would destroy the community by bureaucracy.

No, they would have to change first.

No, society is sick and the client may not be and should be assisted in adjusting to a hostile environment.

Acceptance and respect by the larger mental health system is important for reasons of funding, client referral, and education and consultation work with providers. Center personnel state they are making a positive impact on the larger mental health system.

The centers maintain positive images in their gay communities. The Seattle and Persad centers are the most stable gay institutions in their respective communities. With some exceptions for atypical centers—Neighborhood Counseling, St. Louis Women's Counseling Center, and Chicago Counseling and Psychotherapy Center—centers drew board of directors members from both inside and outside the gay community.

Acceptance and respect for oneself as a lesbian woman or gay man is a large part of the reason for alternative, gay mental health services. Gays reject society's sick stereotype of themselves, seek to remove the burdens and stigma foisted on them, and to build a sense of their own uniqueness, wholeness, place in and contribution to life. Gay organizations have recognized this need and provided counseling, rap and encounter groups for personal growth and re-socialization. Group members share questions and insights which were left out of their straight socialization. They help each other to orient socially and subculturally to a lesbian/gay lifestyle as a healthy alternative to a sick role in heterosexual society.

How many sexual minorities will seek counseling at community mental health centers? We don't know. Why would they go there, rather than to a gay-oriented service? Perhaps, they may do so out of ignorance of gay mental health services. Perhaps, they purposely seek counseling not connected to sexual identity, orientation, and lesbian/gay lifestyle issues.

A third reason that sexual minorities might seek counseling at non-gay agencies, is that they fear embarrassment at being seen at a gay counseling center and identified as a sexual minority person.

Fourth, they may fear counseling. Some clients may choose a strategy of dealing with fears sequentially—counseling first, the gay issue later.

Many of the clients who seek counseling at community mental health centers or with straight (heterosexual), private therapists will not have "come out" as a sexual minority person. They may try to change themselves and deny their feelings toward same-sex individuals. They may have been led to believe that such a change is both possible and desirable. They may deal with this issue in therapy with their non-sexual minority therapist.

Therefore, it is important that the therapist in the community mental health center or other counseling setting know how to deal with sexual preference issues. It is important that the therapist take a non-judgmental, supportive attitude.[16] It is important for the lesbian woman or gay man to accept themselves and to make a health adjustment to lesbian/gay life.[17]

It is not the therapist's job to attempt to dissuade the person from a lesbian or gay identification or to change them, no matter how well-intentioned the therapist might be and the client willing to commit identity suicide. If the person is a lesbian or gay man, they will always have to deal with being who they are—ignoring it will only prolong the pain—for both the client and the therapist. Many such unhappy pairs have gone through years of agonizing therapy at untold costs financially and emotionally. Such persons will have negative memories about the experience. This is how beliefs and feelings about straight (non-gay) psychotherapy get generated.

[1] Laud Humphreys, "Exodus and Identity: The Emerging Gay Culture," Gay Men, (New York: Harper and Row, 1979)

[2] "Come out of the closet" — This is frequently used, although with lack of definitional clarity. The term "closet" refers to a closed or undivulged state regarding one's homosexuality. This may mean homosexual latency in which one's sexuality is unacknowledged to oneself or others, or it may refer to subcultural or cultural levels.

[3] Denyse Lockard, "The Lesbian Community, An Anthropological Approach," The Many Faces of Homosexuality, New York: Harrington Park Press (1986), 84

[4] Ibid., 84

[5] Ibid., 86

[6] Ibid., 86

[7] Court and ball scene — This refers to a sector of gay, largely male, life, whose activities and forms of expression include drag shows (men dressed as and giving performances mimicking women), and drag balls (dances). It's the glitz and glamor, the "gay Hollywood." Some view this as anachronistic in terms of sex roles and offensive to women. Kenneth Read (1980) has studied this as symbol and ritual and a commentary on and ridiculing of societal sex roles.

[8] Even gay persons who are "separatists" from the larger culture relate in various ways, for example, in the marketplace through payment of taxes.

[9] "Homophile" means love of the same.

[10] Foster Gunnison, "The Homophile Movement in America," The Same Sex, (New York: Pilgrim Press, 1969)

[11] A zap is a strategy of political action, specifically a public confrontation technique to obtain a desired goal. Political application began in the 1960s and was used in civil rights movements.

[12] Howard Brown, Familiar Faces Hidden Lives, The Story of Homosexual Men in America Today (New York: Harcourt, Brace Jovanovich, 1976), 200

[13] Study of gay counseling services over the years has led the author to postulate a model of the development processes by which this gap is traversed.

[14] The exception is the Neighborhood Counseling Center, which was described as "an innovative part of the mental health establishment." The situation was one in which there was a gay women and man on the staff of a hospital outpatient clinic which provided outreach into the gay community. Neighborhood cooperated with Gay Community Services, a more typical gay community counseling service.

[15] Alternative centers are alternative in the sense that they cater specifically to a minority subcultural population. While services provided may be similar to those of established institutions in many respects, there are distinctive features as well. In gay counseling services, special values, attitudes, bodies of knowledge, and subcultural styles occur. Changes in the subculture are reflected by changes in the counseling services.

[16] Although there is some disagreement among psychologists as to whether sexual preference is or is not a choice, regardless of the answer, the most constructive approach is non-judgmental. It gives the person freedom to deal with something — regardless of the issue. Counseling takes a non-judgmental approach:
> Acceptance and respect from a counselor allow clients to look at
> themselves and their choices in a more pragmatic, less pessimistic way.
> (Linda Scheffler, Help Thy Neighbor, How Counseling Works and

> When It Doesn't (New York: Grove Press, Inc., 1984), 152

[17] A good book to read (see the Select Reading List in Appendix E) written by Dr. Don Clark, a gay therapist, is Loving Someone Gay.

CHAPTER 4

"If I am not for myself, who will be for me? If I'm only for myself, what am I? If not now, when?

— Hillel, Mishneh: Ethics of the Fathers, 1.14

LESBIAN/GAY MENTAL HEALTH INSTITUTIONS

Erroneous theories and application of physically or psychologically damaging ''cures'' have led gays to form their own mental health delivery systems which recognize the gay person's legitimate mental health needs without assuming gayness is in itself a sickness.

Various kinds of places offer lesbian/gay counseling, such as gay organizations, college groups and women's counseling centers. Those focused on here are services which specifically and primarily serve lesbian/gay clients.[1] Although some of these services serve other sexual minorities as well, their commonality is a lesbian/gay target population.

Gay counseling services occur especially in the major cities on the coasts. Less development in the central plains and south may be related to greater conservatism in general and specifically with regard to gays. Services also began earlier in more progressive places. Communication between centers has tended to cluster on the coasts, including an east coast attempt to form a regional association. On the west coast, personnel visited between centers, resulting in some similarity of services. In the mid-1970s, east coast services tended more to an intellectual approach, while west coast services were influenced by the human potential movement. At the time, the Midwest had few good services, and has developed since then.

Gay counseling services were begun through the valiant efforts of individuals with such personal characteristics as foresight, energy, ability and dedication. They recruited other talented individuals, wrote grants, made organizations work, developed credibility in the gay and larger communities, and did whatever it took to get the endeavor off and running. They began without support from the larger society and mental health system, facing many barriers and a dearth of funds. This pattern is not unusual for fledgling nonprofit organizations trying to get a foothold.

Some centers were basically started by an individual. Pittsburgh's Persad Center was founded in 1972 by a man intending to serve the mental health needs of Pittsburgh's gay population. He successfully applied for government money and opened the Center.

East Bay Gay of Oakland, California was formed in 1973. By 1974 it was pared down to files located in one man's apartment. He was skilled in grant writing and got a $50,000 grant with which to start the Pacific Center for Human Growth.

Seattle Counseling Service for Sexual Minorities was initiated by a doctor who quickly recruited the support of other individuals and the Dorian Society, a gay homophile organization.

Most centers developed out of existing gay movement organizations. The parent organization initially might have provided a name, perspective, space, finances and personnel for the counseling function. Eventually the counseling program developed into adulthood and differentiated out as an independent entity.

The Los Angeles Gay Community Services Center was an outgrowth of the gay movement for social change. It started with brainstorming sessions by some political activists who laid out a sixty to seventy page blueprint for the Center. The founders included a visionary, an organizer, a "people person," a person who knew conventional agencies, and a "nuts and bolts person."

The Gay Liberation Front was operating in Los Angeles in the late 1960s. It started doing counseling in homes. The GLF led into social services in more than one city on the west coast. The Gay Liberation Front influence on the Gay Community Services Center in Los Angeles is reflected in the Center's political philosophy. As was the case with GLF, GCSC has struggled with questions of sexism, racism, and classism over the years. Many of the GCSC staff members were anti-capitalist and supportive of radical psychology, according to which society is viewed as at fault for peoples' problems.

Therapy itself is viewed as an oppressive institution preventive of a thoroughgoing solution involving radical societal change (see Glenn and Kunnes, 1973). Significantly, the radical psychology movement was based in California.

In San Diego, The Gay Liberation Front as well as Metropolitan Community Church's Crisis Intervention Center maintained the Gay Information Service, a counseling hotline. Some GLF members, one person in particular, developed the Gay Center for Social Services.

Philadelphia's Eromin Center received impetus from the Gay Activist Alliance and then differentiated out as an independent entity. It started in an apartment, then got a condemned building from the Society of Friends. A coffee house was operated in the basement while counseling was done upstairs. With a grant of $20,000 from the Van Ameringen Foundation of New York, the Center moved into its own offices in a modern, two story building.

Some centers received their impetus from other centers. An informant at the Los Angeles GCSC claimed that the Center was the model for a number of other centers, including the following: Gay Community Services Center of San Antonio, Texas Free Clinic, Gay Center for Social Services of San Diego, Gay Community Service Center of Sacramento and East Bay Gay of Oakland and Berkeley. Other centers mentioned outside the western area include the Gay Men's VD Clinic and Gay Switchboard of Washington D.C. and the Gay Community Service Center of Buffalo.

Whatever the nature of their genesis, the centers invariably developed and grew. Their client load, staff, programs and funding levels increased. Along with these changes came more formal operating systems. A significant factor leading to formal systematization and bureaucratization is affiliation with the larger mental health system and government.

As centers grew and gained credibility as professional mental health agencies, many turned to and were able to get public funding. Some initially hesitant centers which preferred not to affiliate with the government, fearing the strings attached, later did so out of financial need.

The relationship between gay counseling services and mainstream agencies and government has been a tenuous, twilight existence between acceptance and annihilation. Gay counseling services had the bizarre role of changing the system of which they were becoming a part, while the government was buying them out of their more direct forms of action as change agents through education and political participation. Gay counseling services and the government were accommodating each other.

Through persistent struggle, many gay counseling services succeeded in gaining credibility and a foothold in the larger mental health system. This enabled economic survival and a chance at influencing the larger system.

The direction of change for gay counseling services was increased importance of material incentives relative to goal incentives of the gay movement. The evolution of more structured and formal systems internally was accompanied by adherence to government guidelines externally.

While there was general agreement on basic counseling philosophy and the alternative nature of gay counseling services, much debate surrounded internal issues of government affiliation and politics. Included in this array of concerns were hierarchal versus collective structure, bureaucratization, sexism, racism, classism, and political activism.

Despite the debate about hierarchal versus collective organization, most of the centers were fairly traditional in structure, with boards of directors, administrative positions and division into programs. The exceptions were the George Henry Foundation with its one staff member, and the St. Louis Women's Counseling Center, which operated on a collective, consensus model, a form which occurs more often in women's than in mixed sex, gay organizations.

There are differences of opinion between and within centers concerning the relative status, power and pay distinctions or lack thereof between staff members doing different jobs.

Although concerns with sexism, racism and classism are definitely part of the milieu of most gay counseling services, the actual results are often unimpressive. Most centers reported little effort to attract racial minorities and these efforts were largely unsuccessful.

Many of the centers evidence awareness of the needs of poor clients and do not charge client fees, but little specific outreach was done. Clients who can afford to pay or can pay more for their services have the option and often go to private, gay therapists.

More importance was placed on attracting and encouraging women's participation. The centers varied in their sensitivity and success in this. While at least five of the centers were decidedly male-dominated at the time of the survey, Eromin had more female than male participation of both clients and staff, and Persad required that counselors be feminists.

Concomitant with government funding came formal and hierarchal structures and government rules and regulations, increased record-keeping, paid staff positions, more degreed staff, agency directors and boards of directors. Continual stress to maintain and develop funding resulted in increased numbers of paid administrative staff, who strove to maintain funding for their positions as well as for physical plant, programs, and supplies.

Negative aspects of government funding might be considered to be the loss of full ownership of the services and the imposition of government authority. Nevertheless, the sexual minority communities continued to feel a great deal of ownership for these subcultural institutions. The government priority of serving the severely disturbed client and de-emphasizing services for personal and interpersonal growth and socialization proved not to be disastrous as centers continued to serve a broad client base.

Said one SCS client:

> Relying on the federal government, state or even county funding ultimately leaves you at the mercy of politicians, aspiring policeman/politicians, or a tax revolt. To turn into a profit-oriented agency could cut off access to the people who may need you most but can't afford it. I admire and respect your efforts to deal with people and funding.

Positive aspects of government funding were a more organized, professional approach and the provision of a source of income for staff workers. Paid employment enabled staff to make longer time commitments and provided the incentive to perform the jobs volunteers hesitate to take on, such as record-keeping.

When government as well as private foundation monies tightened up in the late 1970s and 1980s, some services struggled to become more self-reliant through charging or increasing client fees. Some were able to obtain state licensing for third-party payments from the government and insurance companies. The centers applied for tax-exempt status. Other sources of funding included fund-raisers, donations, pledges and social events.

Those centers which received government funding both enjoyed and suffered the consequences. While funding provided a boost it also made centers vulnerable to losing the funding. Such was the case with Persad Center. Persad's $15,000 annual county funding was cut off, causing financial distress. Persad sued the two out of three county commissioners who were responsible. Persad was supported in its struggle by a whole host of public bodies and professional organizations.[2] Petitions with thousands of signatures were sent to the commissioners, and the Governor's Office and Regional Office of the State Department of Welfare appealed to them. It was the first time funding had been cut over the board's recommendations. Probably the two commissioners were out of step with the board and the community: the commissioners chose to hit Persad as the weakest link in the system.

Persad lost its court battle in a legally correct if unjust decision. The ruling was based on the nonexistence of a right of agencies, as distinguished from individuals, to any government funds. Although clients might have successfully sued, funding could then have been awarded to another resource and not to Persad or a gay counseling service.

Persad survived but was not unaffected. Each program had to pay for itself. Overhead was cut by moving into a smaller place, and the paid secretary was laid off. The staff got a proportion of funds brought in, which supported seven part-time professionals.

The Gay Community Social Services Center's experience held out a warning and lesson to other gay centers across the country that getting rich quick has its problems. Money and size require efficient organization and management, and internal problems of sexism, racism and classism were stress points where organizational breakdown could occur.

GCSC began in 1971 in an eleven-room house for which staff sometimes had to panhandle the $250 rent payment. The Center grew quickly to a 1972 budget of $40,000 and a 1973 budget of almost $70,000. Then with approval of tax exempt status and unprecedented, large federal and county government grants to a gay agency, the budget climbed to almost half a million dollars in a period of four months.

However, the program grants did not apply to overhead costs. The large Alcoholism Project for Women grant brought out conflicts within GCSC. The money was earmarked for the program alone, and while the women desired separation from GCSC, the unpaid, central administrators felt they deserved a share of the funds.

Financial, structural and personnel problems led to a severe crisis in 1974 and 1975 which threatened the existence of the Center. Center survival was threatened by a debt of $66,000 including over $15,000 in unpaid salaries, illegal practices and mismanaged records. Women and other workers expressed discontent with the Center administration through picketing, accusations of bossism, and a court case.

The Center managed to survive this incredible mess. The structure changed from a three-person, collective administration module to a larger management collective, then to a co-directorship. The directorship changed hands several times and the Center continued to grow.

Examples of the bureaucratic consequences of government funding are the cases of Gay Community Services of Minneapolis, Boston's Homophile Community Health Service, and Seattle Counseling Service for Sexual Minorities.

Gay Community Services changed from a volunteer organization to a structured, publicly-funded agency. In 1979 the budget was $150,000 and in 1980 it was $230,000. It became one of twenty Hennepin County contracted private programs, with many regulations and record-keeping requirements.

Boston's Homophile Community Health Service was funded mainly by client fees until 1978 when its income doubled with receipt of two government contracts from the Departments of Mental Health and Public Health Division of Alcoholism. The Service struggled to meet government regulations and the increasing red tape that entails, while adequate funding continued to be a problem.

An in-depth examination of the bureaucratic aspects of government funding for Seattle Counseling Service for Sexual Minorities is provided in Chapter 6.

San Francisco has had a lesbian/gay counseling service.

In 1973 Operation Concern began through a fund raiser sponsored by the Tavern Guild. Daffodil was a lesbian/gay group that organized politically concerning mental health issues. Members of the sexual minority community protested the inadequacy of mental health services for their community. As a result, the director of the city's Community Mental Health Services appointed a Gay/Lesbian Mental Health Task Force to assess the situation. There was a centralized unit in the city which had responsibility for making policies about the services. In 1981 special programs were decentralized through the Community Mental Health Services.[3]

An Oakland coffeehouse out of which East Bay Gay Rap started was organized by the Homosexual Action Forum (HAF), which was formalized as an organization in 1969 and which became a branch of the Social Action Research Center. HAF was composed of mostly middle class men who saw a need for counseling services. They tried to change straight agency's attitudes and practices, demanding representation on the board of directors and staff of the Family Service Agency and money from United Bay Area Crusade. They got the San Francisco Mental Health Association to develop a Task Force on Homosexuality and a Gay Caucus in the National Association of Social Work's Golden Gate Chapter.

Gays got onto the staffs of public agencies, including Mission Mental Health, Fort Help, the Center for Special Problems, and the Berkeley Free Clinic. The Center for Special Problems was part of the division of City and County of San Francisco Community Mental Health Services. This Center focused on alcohol/drug abuse and on sex and sexual identity. Getting in the door of established agencies did not mean there were no problems. A Center informant divulged that non-gay staff were pleased when lesbians who were pushing hard on women's issues left.

Chicago had a variety of types of services ranging from the professional Chicago Counseling and Psychotherapy Center and a gay professional service begun by a professional man, to peer gay and lesbian hotlines, pastoral counseling, and the Counseling Resource Center for lesbians. Chicago was the first state to have a consensual law regarding homosexuality back in 1961. The law perhaps resulted in greater gay integration into the society and the use of non-gay therapists. This suggests that gay solidarity and activism is greater where there is greater oppression.

What does a gay counseling service look like?

Inside the old, three-story, poorly-maintained, purplish-gray house with its dirty white posts the semi-grandeur of wooden posts and stairwell, stained glass and bay windows, stained carpets and dowdy donated furniture, all merged into an unkempt comfortableness. Over the fireplace hung an extra thick, hand-hooked rug portrait of Alfred Kinsey. The walls were bulletined with posters, leaflets and index cards announcing forthcoming and past events, house and job seekers; all clearly identified a common gay and counter-cultural set of interests.

There was a room in which several staffers lounged on an old, faded, mauve couch in an office furnished with desks and telephones. Some of the men looked like hippies, long haired, with worn jeans and plaid or variegated colored shirts, boots and accessories. Far fewer in number, one woman was lanky, short haired and wore overalls, and another woman was

SCS 17th Avenue site

ballerinalike, with bunned hair and dressed in a turtleneck shirt and corduroy pants.[4]

These visual perceptions gain depth as the language, meaning, uses, beliefs and all that makes up the culture of the people who work at and use the Seattle Counseling Service for Sexual Minorities is learned. It was six months before one traversed far enough from the cultural understandings with which one began to grasp the new world of meanings, structures and functions of this place, despite being engrossed in doing just that. The newcomer was well advised to proceed slowly. The process was one of small steps and jarring leaps from one set of understandings to another. The Seattle Counseling Service is a veritable conduit between two worlds through which many a traveler has been transposed.

The Service is located on Capitol Hill, one of Seattle's famed seven hills. Capitol Hill is centrally located and not far from downtown Seattle. It has inner city residential structures ranging from glorious mansions and comfortable homes to old and new apartment buildings and condominiums. The older homes are often inhabited by multiple families, collective living groups, or subdivided into apartments or boarding houses. Many gay people and a few gay bars inhabit The Hill and it

SCS 17th Avenue building hearth

is sometimes referred to as The Gay Ghetto. Broadway, the main street, hosts an array of shops and businesses and is noted in some circles as popular among gay strollers.

Seattle's exceptionally beautiful physical environment, along with its adequate cultural environment, earned it the title of America's Most Livable City. On the west it sits above Puget Sound, across whose sometimes gray sometimes sun sparkled waters, dotted with ships and sea gulls, islands rest and snowcapped peaks of the Olympic Range are visible. Twisting waterway canals and a lake link the salt water Sound with fresh water Lake Washington on the eastern side of the City, across and above which other land masses are finally topped by the snowcapped Cascade Range. The sun, when it shines, rises and sets over the mountains while the waters wind around the lands and out to sea.

The Asian International District, antique Pioneer Square with old Seattle buried beneath its streets, the waterfront and seagoing culture, the Space Needle testament to a recreational center remaining from the 1962 Seattle World's Fair, and the Univeristy of Washington highlight Seattle's activity. The development of the arts, entertainment and the proliferation of community organizational life indicate that Seattle has

SCS (left) is torn down when SMHI (right) gets new building.

everything a city needs. Developed and only somewhat overgrown, Seattle can be felt as a whole. Likewise, Seattle's gay community has a feeling of belonging and a sense of itself.

Before the Seattle Counseling Service inhabited the house on Capitol Hill's Sixteenth Avenue, it had been at two successively rented houses on Malden Avenue. Both had foyers, second floors, telephone desks and residents. The second house had more room for counseling. The Service moved as the landlord tore down the buildings rather than make necessary repairs.

The Service had outgrown its place again and moved to the larger and inexpensive Sixteenth Avenue Location in 1973. As with the second Malden Avenue house, the inside of the house had to be entirely painted. Its walls had previously been a canvas for preschoolers. It had a foyer, telephone desks and three floors, with residents living oftentimes on the third floor.

In 1977 the Service had to move to the second floor of a two-story building on the corner of Broadway above an office space. The Sixteenth Avenue landlord, Seattle Mental Health Institute, had agreed with the Capitol Hill Council that in order for SMHI to get its new building, other social service agencies, SCS chief among them, would have to move

Intimate
conversation
in
counseling
room

and its buildings be returned to residential use. So the Service became one floor instead of three, half the feet, double the price, and more professional in its offices instead of a funky, comfy house. It retained the dowdy donated furniture, the hall bulletin boards of in-community messages and the Alfred Kinsey rug. We all cleaned, painted, nailed, hung drapes where the neon gas station sign across the street jumped in the windows, and settled in. The place felt like Seattle Counseling Service.

There was less room, the usual stale and choking pall of cigarette smoke, and the old problem of staff congregating in the telephone room where it was supposed to be quiet for counseling. So we made the interior decorating changes as usual and experimented with how six paid and thirty-five volunteer staff members could sit at three desks and two telephone stalls without getting in the clients' way. The men had cut their hair and shaved and staff members looked somewhat more like busy social workers than relaxed counter-culturals. The 1960s and early 1970s counter-culture had had its heyday and been replaced.

The Service changed, marking off eras in its developmental life while its essence and raison d'etre remained intact.

SCS community bulletin board

The Seattle Counseling Service for Sexual Minorities was the first such institution in the United States. It began in Seattle, Washington in 1969. Edward Lindaman, futurist, former President of Whitworth College in Spokane, Washington, said that the Pacific Northwest is a place that attracts people. In the past people were known for where they came from. In the future, Lindaman said, people will be known for where they're drawn to. In the latter 1960s and 1970s many people came to Seattle. Their energy and that generated by the mixture of people combined to make Seattle a dynamic place.

Seattle has had numbers of firsts, in the areas of progressive politics and human services. However, in the last decade, Washington State has had the dubious distinction of ranking last and fourth from last for per capita expenditure of mental health funds.

This book presents a detailed look at what has been happening at Seattle Counseling Service. All of the changes with the times can be seen to have occurred over the existence of this first and longest-lived agency.

Other lesbian/gay counseling services soon followed on the heels of the Seattle Service. They were responding to the same

Staff member preparing the new building

set of forces giving rise to this sudden mushrooming of gay services in the same relative time-frame around the country. Other minority and women's communities spawned human services centers during this period as well. An in-depth study of the Seattle Service gives us insight into these general and specific forces at work.

This is the first history of lesbian/gay counseling services and it is important to some people. For those who plan, make policy and administer mental health services, it should become important. While it's important for Seattle to study this service, it's also important for other areas of the country—for making comparisons, gauging successes and failures, and learning how to get started, how to manage an organizaiton and its growth, and how to reach and maintain a delicate balance in its relationship to the lesbian/gay community on the one hand and the larger mental health system, government funding, and society on the other.

The history of Seattle Counseling Service (SCS) can be conceptualized in a four-period schema. These periods can themselves be related to developments in the gay community locally as well as to currents in the gay movement nationally. The different character of the four periods demonstrates points

SCS Broadway site

made in Chapter 3, namely that the gay subculture is internally diverse and not monolithic, and that it changes over time. The periods can also be related to changes occurring to SCS in relation to the larger mental health system.

The first period in SCS history, from roughly 1969 to 1972, was one in which the moving force was the provision of professional mental health counseling to meet the needs of the gay population. It was a period in which gaining credibility and support from the larger mental health system was of major concern. The physician who founded the Service and other professional persons who were either gay or saw a need for services to gays, were the ones primarily involved with the Service. The Dorian Society was the local, gay community organization closely associated with the Service. The Dorian Society tended to be moderate in perspective and can be seen as part of the Homophile Period of the gay movement.

The second period, effective from 1972 to 1975, dates from the first female directorship through the tripartite coordinator organization. With the female director, more women joined the staff and the female client population climbed. Other client service populations were recognized and grew, especially those related to gender identity. The name was changed from its original name, Seattle Counseling Service for Homosexuals to Seattle Counseling Service for Sexual Minorities. The program went beyond a strictly mental health model. Programs for socialization and situational problems were added. This period occurred at the time of the more militant, Gay Liberation period of the gay movement. Other influences of the times were the hippie, countercultural movement, and the social upheaval surrounding the Vietnam War. SCS tended toward a countercultural, anarchistic style with looser organizational structure and countercultural ideological features. The Service became more politically involved during this period.

The third period, from 1975 to 1977, began with a new, male directorship and a tighter organizational style with more defined staff roles and a combination of hierarchal and democratic features. Like the second period, the third period is politically oriented, though in a different style. The outside community organization which now became influential is a socialist-feminist organization. The multi-issue politics of this organization as well as a confrontational style influenced the character of administrative and political expression that came out of SCS.

The fourth period, from 1977 to 1986, can be characterized as a return to the professional model and a turning away from political involvement and the more radical, political faction. There is a degree of re-association with the more moderate, gay political faction, the new Dorian Group.[5] The hallmark of this period is increasing institutionalization associated with the demands of the King County Board of Mental Health and the State of Washington for complete compliance with new regulations, and an apolitical, mental health model. The directors during this period are professionally trained and oriented.

[1] The data for this chapter is based on two field trips to gay counseling services nationally and attendance at a meeting of directors of east coast gay counseling; a questionnaire, and three follow-up questionnaires and telephone follow-up survey. Nevertheless, not all changes in services are discussed here.

[2] Among its supporters were the Governor, the National Association of Social Workers locally, the Greater Pittsburgh Psychological Association, the county administrator and board of Mental Health Mental Retardation programs, and eighty of the mental health systems in the area.

[3] Jack Rabin, Kathleen Keefe, Michael Burton. "Enhancing Services for Sexual Minority Clients: A Community Health Approach, Social Work, Volume 31, No. 4, July through August 1986, p 294

[4] Hippie garb was big in the 1970s and this was the predominant theme in dress.

[5] "Dorian Group" took its name in 1975 as a spinoff from the "Dorian Society," which took its name in 1969. The Dorian Society was involved in the beginning of SCS. The name "Dorian" is a spinoff from the Dorians in Crete — where, according to the book, Eros, the first recorded act of an account of sodomy, used as part of a puberty rite, was made. The thread of continuity is Mr. Charles Brydon, a long-time, Seattle gay activist, who named these organizations. This information is from personal communication with Charlie, 1986.

CHAPTER 5

''It's a lot easier to go in and get help when you know you won't be condemned for who or what you are.''

— Client

THE
NITTY-GRITTY
HISTORY

he following detailed history of the first and oldest gay counseling service is based on an ethnography[1] of Seattle Counseling Service for Sexual Minorities. It illustrates how such a service starts, the social-cultural and specifically political forces at work and how these get played out in the course of the services' development and interaction with larger societal representatives. This history illustrates how and why counseling services for lesbians and gays have been successful. Lesbian/gay counseling services are doing the job effectively and other mental health personnel can learn from this.

Another source worth consulting, which focuses on the organizational problems of gay counseling services is an article by John Gonsiorek.[2] He makes many astute observations which he says is "highly impressionistic and descriptive." The purpose of this history is not to focus on problems but to provide an overall description and analysis.

This is written for a diversity of audiences, including anthropologists, sociologists, psychologists, social workers;

planners and administrators; medical historians; and activists, community organizers and service providers for women, racial and sexual minorities rights and welfare.

Anthropologists typically refer to the people with whom they live and work as "my people." They seek to establish rapport with the people, and through this unique and personal relationship, to produce ethnographies which illuminate the internal meaning of a culture and what it feels like to be a member of it. This study represents an anthropologist's and insider's view.

Historians will find the oral history and document techniques used in this study to be familiar. The material on gay counseling services and the gay movement in historical context and developmental sequences in the gay movement and gay counseling services should be of interest.

Political scientists will be particularly interested in the politics of the gay movement, the various political approaches and strategies used over time in dealing with the mainstream society, and the details of the relationship presented in the case study of Seattle Counseling Service and King County/Washington State. Interesting governmental behaviors vis-a-vis a stigmatized minority population are revealed.

Medical historians can add the information on gay counseling services and the gay mental health movement to their account of the history of medicine in this country. Perhaps light will be shed on and perspective added to their understanding of the role of intra-cultural difference in health care.

Mental health students, practitioners, planners and administrators will find discussion and light thrown on their concerns with issues of gay mental health, counseling style and philosophy, integrated and separate services, alternative services and their relationship to the mental health system, and funding. Mental health personnel will gain insights into what is going on and what works when it comes to providing services to gays, (and to other subcultural minorities). Lesbians, gay men, other women, and ethnic/racial minority activists, community organizers and service providers will find some familiar and perhaps some new ideas and techniques.

This section may also appeal to someone looking for a good story. If you do not have an interest in the detailed history section, skip it and go on.

The following section is the history of the Seattle gay counseling institution.

The data was largely collected over a seven-year period, from 1973 to 1980. There were three follow-up questionnaires, a telephone survey, and interview in the years 1980 to 1986. The author was on-site at Seattle Counseling Service for seven years as a working member of the staff. This provided a unique vantage point from which to go beyond the establishment of rapport and an outsider's inside view. The author was a social scientist and an insider. The approach, methodologies and techniques utilized in this study are many and diverse including: qualitative and quantitative, social and cultural approaches; case study, diachronic (historical) and statistical methodologies; documentation, questionnaire, oral history, interview, and participant observation techniques. Participant observation was also carried out in the surrounding community throughout the research period.

As indicated in the previous chapter, four periods have been identified in the history of Seattle Counseling Service for Sexual Minorities: homophile; gay liberation; socialist-feminist, and professional.

The First Period: The Homophile Period (1969-1972)

The idea to start the Seattle Service dates back to 1968 when the need for such a service became apparent to a medical doctor working at the University of Washington. He was studying male prostitutes, some of whom were gay, and found gay youth prostitution to be related to lack of other means of financial support. He was interested in finding the youth employment and also recognized their need for more counseling.

The physician was called on to do counseling at a rate of one or more times a day by gay persons who often had negative experiences with psychiatrists. They reported the psychiatrists' treatment had not been helpful, that they lacked interest in or knowledge about homosexuality, or had a moralistic attitude.

The physician did not know where to send the increasing number of people who called him. The Chairman of the Psychiatry Department at the University of Washington suggested that he set up a counseling center, which the Doctor agreed was a good idea. To get money he wrote to the Erickson Foundation of Baton Rouge, Louisiana. Almost immediately, Erickson sent $3600 in seed money to be administered through the University. The second year the doctor requested $2400 — since Erickson had indicated its intention to reduce and discontinue its seed allocation — and got $900. The Dorian Society contributed $1000, largely earned from an auction in the gay community. The money paid for renting a house, the telephone and utilities.

The Service associated closely with the Dorian Society, a small homophile organization founded in 1967 and predominantly comprised of middle class professional and business men. Until February 1970, the Service was called the Dorian Counseling Service at Dorian House.

Some persons were affiliated with the Counseling Service as distinct from the Dorian Society. A graduate student who had worked with the physician on the prostitution study did much of the actual legwork involved in getting the Service started.

Many of the telephone counselors were recruited from the Dorian Society. University students training in psychology, medicine and social work were recruited to do in-person counseling, while volunteer psychiatrists acted as consultants. During this first period there was a definite functional and status differential between telephone counselors and nonprofessional staff members, and in-person counselors who were mental health professionals.

A resident lived at the Service, exchanging a nighttime counseling presence for room and board and later, a small monthly salary. The resident's role was an important one. He maintained the building and was basically responsible for its functioning. He handled the telephone calls at night, often of an emergency nature, and filled in evening phone shifts when no one else was doing it. An older, retired man was the first resident. Residents were often University students. One resident who survived for the longest time before "burning out," practically acted as director for a time. He worked very hard and felt a sense of responsibility to continuing the job because someone had to do it. He left when the female director took over and became resident. She was joined by a woman and man, and later by three other residents, living in the second Malden Avenue and Sixteenth Avenue houses.

The founding doctor had been the director for the first year. His time was limited by other activities however. A priest acted as a coordinator for nine months. A graduate student was made the acting director and the physician still held the title of director. The acting director left out of dissatisfaction with this situation.

The Service and the Dorian Society disassociated in 1970. The Dorian Society was primarily a social club while the Service was concerned with accountability and credibility from a mental health standpoint. The use of space and personnel became incompatible. It was particularly feared that closeted clients would be discouraged by the overtly homosexual social presence of Dorian. On the other hand, there was some feeling that dissociation would alienate the homophile community who would take it as a repudiation of working with homophile organizations, not to mention the monthly rent contribution paid by the Dorian Society. So there were considerations and growing pains with the break.

The Service was bent on gaining respect from the larger mental health community and getting funding from it as well. The Erickson Foundation had only provided seed money and it was necessary to seek another source of funding. The founding director was a member of the King County Board of Mental Health (KCBMH) and requested funding from it in 1970. He got $2250 for the first six months and $2250 for the second six months. This money enabled the Service to pay rent, utilities, supplies, maintenance costs and some minimal salaries.

The Second Period: The Gay Liberation Period (1972-1975)

In May of 1971 a woman was appointed the director. The physician became the executive director while she did the actual administration of the Service. She had been at the Service since 1970 as a volunteer, during which time her level of familiarity and commitment developed. The first change related to the fact that the new director was a woman in what had been a male-dominated agency. Some men were unable to deal with a female director. On the other hand, more women came on board, both staff and clients.

A psychologist by training, this director counseled more seriously disturbed clients. She also further developed the record-keeping and communications systems. In the latter sense she was institutionalizing the Service. She did so in response to the increasing size of SCS, which necessitated more formal, written procedures and systematization. Previously oral communications were replaced by written communications. She was aware of taking steps toward institutionalization, and anticipated future development along these lines, without however anticipating the intervening, more politically oriented period.

In another sense, institutionalization was resisted. Rules and regulations were not emphasized, and there was a wariness and resistance to receiving public money. The major fear was one of losing client confidentiality. At the time, the government wanted client information of an identifying nature. A double standard existed in that although private counseling was allowed to be confidential, publicly-funded counseling was not. Eventually an awareness of the confidentiality issue developed in the mental health system as a whole.

The name change from Seattle Counseling Service for Homosexuals to Seattle Counseling Service for Sexual Minorities, formally established in 1973, took a year. It reflected the growing number of other-than-gay sexual minority clients, especially transvestites and transgenderals. There were some clients dealing with sadomasochism. Their concern was often related to role identity, in that heterosexually-oriented male masochists might wonder whether they were gay. SCS was the most suitable place for these client populations to come. The client base of the Service was widening in concept and practice, having started with male gay youth prostitutes, and expanded to other gays, lesbian women, and other sexual minorities. Heterosexuals dealing with sex-related issues have also come to SCS, since it was the only agency at the time which was dealing with sexual issues.

The director resigned in the spring of 1973. She[3] was uninterested in being part of an increasingly institutionalized setting from which the early innovators were leaving. She went on to found another innovative organization concerned with women's sexuality. A system of three co-directors or coordinators came into being in October 1973 to fill the leadership vacuum. They were responsible for the aspects of administration, program, and volunteers, and each had a small collective or committee. These small collectives were part of the larger staff collective. This latter collective met weekly to decide the philosophic and detailed running matters of the agency.

During this period SCS tended toward a counter-cultural and anarchistic style with looser organizational structure and counter-cultural ideological features. The hippie, counter-cultural movement was pervasive at the time and influenced the Service.

The trend during the second period can be viewed in the context of developments in the gay movement locally and nationally. Seattle had one of the earliest of the Gay Liberation Front organizations started in late 1969. It espoused that gays change society rather than adjust to it. It also formulated the relation of the gay struggle to the struggles of women, racial, and other sexual minorities. It can be thought of as also related to the widespread social unrest and militancy surrounding the Vietnam War.

Some old Gay Liberation Front members had joined the staff during this period, radicalizing the Service. SCS took a strong stand opposing the War. The political facet was reflected in service provision. Draft counseling resulted in perhaps eight to ten gay persons being assisted in getting honorable discharges from the Armed Forces. Letters written by SCS requested discharges without however stating that they be granted based on gayness as a disability. Abortion referral, seen as related to the women's movement, was also available.

The tripartite organization ran into problems. Disorganization became increasingly apparent; questions of sexism, racism and classism were strongly felt and debated. The stresses of SCS as a live-in collective of residents versus a service delivery function for use by staff and clients mounted; tensions between primary staff persons were rife and one of the coordinators resigned. Other central staff members were barely hanging on. Some stayed out of a sense of responsibility to the Service to achieve organizational stability before leaving. Grants were sought to provide a more stable financial base. Part of the staff "burnout" phenomenon was related to the need for payment. There were questions as to whether the necessary money to keep the place and personnel going would come from grants, gay community donations, or client fee for services.

The tripartite structure was dissolved. The other two coordinators left in turn. New leadership was needed. Two persons were approved as co-coordinators, and the organization functioned with the collective staff group having the main decision-making power.

The Service was under criticism from some of the more moderate individuals who had previously been involved or dissociated from SCS because of its changed style. This included the founding doctor. The critics felt SCS had lost its credibility as a mental health agency. They also felt that SCS no longer attracted or served the entire sexual minority population in need of services. Specifically they felt that poorer, counter-cultural people were favored while the older, more middle class, moderate people were dissuaded from using the Service by its radical and countercultural style.

Another major factor affecting the composition of both staff and the client population was the split between gay women and men, which was well under way locally and nationally. The feminist and lesbian feminist movements had raised women's consciousness about the secondary status of women in the gay movement and its organizations.

The question of sexism at SCS was a wrenching one. Of the small number of women, a few left the Service. A call was put out by some "separatist" oriented women in the community for remaining women to leave, while a socialist-feminist faction thought women should hold their ground. A meeting of two core staff women and non-staff women was called by a staff woman. It ended with the few remaining SCS women stating their case and choosing to stay. Nevertheless, continual struggle and special efforts were necessary to get women's participation as staff and clients during this period.

Along with the proliferation of gay organizations occurring all over the country, alternatives for gay and lesbian counseling developed in Seattle, including a more middle class oriented, private counseling group, and a lesbian center which offered peer counseling. The smorgasbord of alternative service providers was effectively able to serve the diverse sectors of a differentiating gay and sexual minority community.

The Service was also being used as a drop-in center by some people, especially between late 1972 and the spring of 1974, after the first Gay Community Center in Seattle closed in the fall of 1972.

In order to provide another place for people to socialize, SCS encouraged the formation of the second Gay

Community Center, which opened in May 1974 in a house next door to SCS. This allowed SCS to re-specialize as a mental health service. It no longer had to meet a dual need in being a social center as well. Furthermore, the two functions were considered to be incompatible. The concern was that clients would be put off by entering into a social situation on the way to getting therapy. This situation also exacerbated problems of client confidentiality within the gay community.

With funding from the King County Board of Mental Health, SCS became part of the larger mental health system and connected to the county, state and federal governments. The Comprehensive Mental Health Care Act of 1965 primarily operates through the Comprehensive Mental Health Care Centers. These Centers are spread over the country, each covering a catchment area from which it derives and serves clients. The philosophy of this system is to have local and comprehensive centers rather than a piecemeal approach to the delivery of mental health services.

Seattle Counseling Service is not a Comprehensive Mental Health Care Center and was to affiliate with either Harborview Hospital or Seattle Mental Health Institute, the Community Mental Health Care Center for the Capitol Hill area. It was felt that the Service's identity could best be maintained through affiliation with SMHI. SCS made application to SMHI, which submitted the SCS proposal for funding along with a request for matching funds for itself from King County. SMHI subcontracted with SCS to provide services to sexual minorities and consultation and information to the community within the SMHI catchment area.

In return, SMHI was to provide mental health backup services, including day treatment, vocational rehabilitation and emergency services to SCS clients resident in the area. Each agency would refer clients to the other as appropriate.

In addition, SMHI was to administer the King County funds to SCS and to monitor its services and records, which would be inspected and audited by SMHI and State personnel. SMHI had the right to cut off funds if SCS records were not found to be up to par. The contract with SMHI was to continue through December 1973, at which time it could be renewed or amended.

More money ($600,000) became available in Washington State for mental health and all the King County-funded agencies requested increased budgets. SCS proposed a larger budget in the amount of $19,442, the second smallest request of all the agencies. Seattle Mental Health Institute had however declined to endorse the new budget request. It was willing only to do the financial paperwork but no longer to be responsible for monitoring SCS. The money was granted in December 1973 and SCS became a directly County funded agency rather than affiliate of SMHI. The struggle to maintain this status became a continuing saga and major concern of the Service.

While welcomed, reliance on government funding brought attendant fears: invasion of privacy and government surveillance around the issue of client records; bureaucracy; increased dependence on salaries; and a more developed superstructure dependent on the continuation of funding. On the one hand, staff worried about being co-opted by the established system. On the other hand, they worried about the risk of being left high and dry should funding be revoked.

The King County Board of Mental Health (KCBMH) did a site visit in November 1973, at which time their concerns were evidenced. They questioned the need for the additional money, and said there was not enough to go around. SCS staff replied that it was now necessary that they be paid. The site team said the national directive was for increased volunteerism and questioned the effect payment of SCS workers would have on mental health workers at other agencies. They also mentioned their concerns about funding in the future, gay community inter-agency relations, SCS' division of labor and the fact that another gay agency had applied for mental health money. The staff responded that the relation between gay agencies was one of cooperation and that each occupied a different niche in the community.

The increased money went to staff salaries. A small amount of it was divided among many staff members who worked twenty-five or more hours per week according to expression of their financial need. The division of money among many workers rather than a single large director's salary was a choice argued for with the site team, one of whose more supportive members helped by likening this form to the Grinnel model of team therapy. SCS chose this system for philosophic/political reasons that revolved around notions of worker equality, and simply because of the need for more workers to be paid and the impracticability of having only one paid worker.

Salaried work came at a time when various factors called for it. The volunteers were largely unemployed and donating a large part of their time to SCS. The fashionableness of 1960s hippie poverty had passed, times were getting harder, requiring more money, and people wanted to be paid for their work. It was not a hobby; it was a full-time job to provide serious services and keep SCS going. The Service was growing, requiring greater time and energy inputs. The government financial connection of itself necessitated significant increases in organization and paperwork. This type of work was not the kind people were likely to volunteer to do on a stable continuing basis.

111

The Third Period: The Socialist-Feminist Period (1975-1977)

The third period was ushered in when the County required that SCS structure be tightened up for 1975 with a director and separation of staff and members of the board of directors. Much of this period consisted of the struggle with the King County Board of Mental Health (KCBMH), which is detailed in the next chapter.

The Fourth Period: The Professional Period: (1977-1986)

In the fourth period three women directors steered SCS in a professional, mental health direction. The board of directors also became more active in this. The board had become the policy-making body par excellence and its members actively participated in agency work as well at this point.

The new director was hired in June 1977. She had been a volunteer and was entering graduate school to become a professional social work administrator. The fact that she was a woman and black was seen in a positive light, while some questioned her lack of gay identification. She was not involved in movement politics. She had a managerial style of administration, hierarchal and not democratic. The administrative staff now submitted weekly written work reports to her and periodically met for staff development and planning sessions rather than the regular staff meetings and ongoing group decision-making of the previous period. The decision-making power of the board of directors was increased and that of the administrative and volunteer staff decreased.

The director's energy and approach were very effective in dealing with the County's funding cutoff. Her appeal and a concerted effort to meet their demands resulted in a successful recovery of support. The effectiveness of her directorship was short-lived, however, as other demands on her time overtook the amount of energy she devoted to SCS. Eventually the administrative staff called this to the attention of the board. In January 1978 another staff woman took on the clinical aspect of the directorship and in May the director resigned. The other woman became full-time acting director and was made permanent director in October, a position she held for eight years until stepping down.

It was 1978 and the flavor for the next eight years was established during the longest directorship in the history of the SCS.

Under this new director SCS enjoyed good relations with King County. The clinical program and record-keeping system were tightened up appreciably, especially with the full-time work of a capable, professional, staff social-worker. After a long process, SCS had become an established part of the larger mental health system, a system which was becoming increasingly bureaucratized. The director resigned in 1985 and the Clinical Director became Director. The up-to-date story of SCS in 1985 to 1986 will be told in chapter 8.

The professional period has been a long one and continues. SCS seems to have stabilized with this identity. However, the pace of growth and change has been stepped up by the new director. Professionalism and bureaucratic development have continued to proceed. SCS is larger, with more programs and organization.

[1] An "ethnography" or "ethnographic study" is a term in anthropology for a detailed description of a culture. This ethnography was originally done by the author for a Ph.D. thesis at the University of Pittsburgh in th 1970s.

[2] John Gonsiorek, "Organizationl and Staff Problems in Gay/Lesbian Mental Health Agencies," A Guide to Psychotherapy with Gay and Lesbian Clients (New York: Harrington Park Press, 1985)

[3] She stated this to the author in a personal communication in the late 1970s.

114

CHAPTER

6

"Society at large produces the problem for sexual minorities and should bear the responsibility of easing their pain and reducing the problem."

— Client

GROWTH

WITHOUT

COOPTATION

This is a detailed story of interactions between SCS and KCBMH. It chronicles the character of site-visits and evaluations of SCS, the struggle SCS waged to retain funding, the increased County demands for accountability and how SCS responded to these. It describes the maneuvers effected by both SCS and KCBMH, the politics of SCS, and a reflection of the politics of KCBMH.

This is a story of the coming together of an alternative agency and a government body through confrontation and mutual accommodation — a story of the growth of SCS' relationship to government without surrendering essential principles of ownership by and service to the sexual minority community and client confidentiality. It illustrates how the benefit of inclusion of minority institutions in the larger mental health system can be done without cooptation. This matter is of sufficient enough importance to alternative agencies to require a separate, detailed chapter to explicate it.

Seattle Counseling Service, by virtue of funding, was part of a bureaucratic system of decision-making and functioning.

The Service was periodically evaluated through site visits by government decision-makers and personnel.

This section[1] describes how SCS evolved in relation to its interaction with the King County Board of Mental Health, which was responsible for funding allocation under the Department of Social and Health Services for this area in Washington State.

The interaction between SCS and KCBMH necessitated a series of internal changes and struggle in SCS. The third period (1975-1977) in SCS history was one of outright struggle and confrontation with KCBMH.[2] It was followed by a fourth period of accommodation. The internal changes that were made resulted in successful compliance with government standards.

In May 1974 a KCBMH site-visit had been done to determine whether funding would be granted from June through December. SCS also submitted a five-year projected budget. The three-member County site-visit team asked questions about the duplication of gay services, referrals and inter-agency cooperation. The team expressed concern that younger, more countercultural clients were being served to the neglect of older, more respectable clients. It asked about agency structure and bookkeeping. It said the government now required that a written policy, a procedure manual, and a needs assessment be done. The team also wanted an annual report on goals and budget and the appointment of an advisory board of persons currently unaffiliated with SCS. The team suggested that SCS might get funding elsewhere and commented about the pressure on them from two other County funded agencies that wanted the money SCS got.

During this period of SCS developmental history, the agency was highly political, whether by the nature of its very existence or activities. The kinds of political participation the Service could lawfully engage in were limited by the Hatch Act. This Act prohibited State funds for nonprofit, tax exempt organizations to be associated with politics. Political participation had to be related to client welfare and advocacy. Lobbying for candidates and legislation was forbidden.

Many relevant and allowable political situations arose, including statewide gay foster care rights, the inclusion of sexual orientation in City fair employment and housing ordinances,[2] women's rights, anti-gay media campaigns, and police-gay relations. SCS staff members were among the respected gay activists who presented testimony at State hearings. Gay foster case became legal and an agency called Youth Advocates handled cases involving gay foster care. SCS staff participated in City hearings, which resulted in the Seattle Fair Employment and Fair Housing Ordinances; and SCS had a regular representative to a feminist coordinating council, which participated in supporting and taking actions on most of the feminist issues of the day. Out of an educational series sponsored by SCS, a specifically gay political organization with a radical, multi-issue political philosophy was created at a time when Seattle lacked a gay political organization. This political organization took on matters outside the limits allowable to SCS.

The director and some other staff and board members of this period of development were heavily involved in radical political activity. The freedom of choice to participate was never lost. Most of the staff were either inactive or participated in other political styles and activities of their choosing. However, it was widely assumed that because certain key individuals were associated with a socialist-feminist political organization, that this represented everyone at SCS. It was even sometimes alleged that the agency was an extension of this political organization. While it is true that the political perspective of this organization, especially the "multi-issue approach," which related the struggle of sexual minorities to those of other minorities, workers and women, had a large influence on the character of SCS during this period, there was never an official affiliation.

Critical attacks on political participation and the style in which it was done came from gay community individuals and factions, from King County, and from some SCS staff and board members. Criticism from the gay community came from persons with a continuing interest in the Service, from the two sectors which had earlier influenced it: both the more moderate faction and some of the more radical, countercultural factions objected. The former were opposed to political participation and saw SCS as a mental health service agency only. The latter objected to the particular affiliation and style of political expression associated with the socialist-feminist organization.

The County funding agent joined in by forbidding SCS from doing political work. Forces within the Service polarized around the political question, with the majority oriented away from political activity. SCS had become a veritable political battlefield. Intense encounters occured between gay community factions and the staff debated politics at meetings. This proved energy draining and disruptive to services.

The director resigned in the spring of 1977 and went into political work. SCS went in the other direction.

Rumor was that SCS' funding had been cut for 1975. A KCBMH supporter of SCS said that six other agencies had submitted inflated budgets and that they were asked to reduce and resubmit them in September, and that SCS might then be reconsidered. As late as October and after repeated attempts by SCS to see the site-visit report, no formal communication had been made about the report. SCS was finally informed by telephone that there would be no money for 1975 and probably no review of the case in September.

Seattle Counseling Service organized a public letter-writing and media campaign to protest the situation and to gain support for continued funding. The community and media responded and KCBMH was deluged with letters from gay and non-gay individuals, agencies and organizations.

A copy of the long-awaited site-visit report finally arrived. It was less than a page long and negative. It was accompanied by a letter from the chair of the Board's Program Review Committee which indicated that the State's involuntary commitment law was impacting the County funding priorities. This referred to the fact that more mentally ill persons would be out of the State Hospitals and into the local communities and community mental health centers, putting a strain on them, since unfortunately, funding was not increased to meet the increased needs.

Seattle Counseling Service attended the November KCBMH meeting with about seventy-five supporters. This was six months after the previous site visit that had resulted in tentative refunding only until the end of the year. Most of them had to wait outside of the overcrowded meeting room. SCS was immediately put on the agenda.

The SCS spokesperson read a prepared statement in which the following remarks were made:

1.   an objection to the procedures used by the Board in relationship to how it handled funding;
2.   a response to the charges made in the site review letter and the countercharge that the review was inaccurate, incomplete and unprofessional; and

3. a defense of SCS as a valid agency having a record of five years' standing with impressive service statistics. The statement also spoke to the Board's responsibility to meet the mental health needs of the entire community, including the sexual minority community, and proposed that a second review be conducted.

Fifteen statements were allowed to follow from attending supporters, including statements from individuals, and members of the mental health community and agency representatives. One individual dramatically described owing her life to SCS.

The Board chairman stated that funds had to be cut since SMHI would not monitor SCS, to which point he was reminded that two other agencies were affiliated with SMHI without being monitored. He also said that the Board did not have adequate information about SCS, to which the spokesperson replied that all requested information had been forwarded. The chairman then agreed to conduct a second site visit and review.

The second review was done in December by an eight-person committee. The financial books were checked thoroughly and questions on organization, services and funding sources were discussed.

An allocation of $9,721 was granted for the first six months of 1975 with the following requirements and contingencies:
1. reorganization of the board of directors to have full authority, to be separate from the staff; having professional as well as citizen membership, and full authority;
2. reorganization of the staff with an executive director to replace the tripartite organization;
3. copies of fee schedules and receipts to be sent to KCBMH every sixty days;

4. a declining funding level with SCS providing $2,916 in the second six months of 1975;

5. documentation of efforts to obtain other sources of revenue;

6. a primary, treatment-oriented focus and not political and community organization.

The contract made further specifications concerning monthly reports and record inspection, with the threat of financial withdrawal for failure to comply. SCS did meet all the requirements and contingencies, and was so acknowledged by KCBMH.

One of the coordinators and actively involved staff person had emerged as a leader and was elected to be the director in January 1975. He and two other staff members had to resign their positions from the board.

The concerns about organizational structure and personnel continued under the new director. A transition was made from a loosely-organized collective to a tighter structure with fixed job positions. Although most staff were in favor of increased organizational tightness, a minority expressed concern over the increasing differences between paid and unpaid staff. The paid or core staff were increasingly visible as a unit differentiated from the staff as a whole. The paid staff were open to criticism from unpaid staff and gay community members, and were held responsible for the Service.

The paid, administrative staff became even more crystallized when additional, paid CETA (Comprehensive Education Training Act)[3] positions started in January 1975. The increased money allowed for redistribution of positions and higher pay. The director position was now the only one paid by County funds. Three persons had CETA positions, and two others were paid as well. Six paid staff in all began forty-hour work weeks. The paid staff had daily, morning staff meetings, while the entire staff met one night per week, alternating business with educational training sessions. The full staff voted on decisions at staff meetings. The administrative staff was expected by itself and others to conduct the full staff meetings, and to take a leadership role.

The administrative staff spent much of its energy on keeping up with the demands of the County funding agent and dealing with a series of challenges to SCS' funded status. Once established, the superstructure found itself in a protracted struggle to maintain itself.

The King County Board of Mental Health conducted its next site visit in April of 1975, at which time SCS was told that the State budget should be resubmitted. At their April 9th meeting, KCBMH adopted a reduced funding formula. SCS was to receive $6,085 of its current allocation for the second six months of 1975 and 50% of its current allocation for all of 1976 ($9,721). SCS was to supply $2,916 in matching funds for the second half of 1975 and $9,721 for 1976.

In fact, in June KCBMH cut SCS funds. A core staff member was laid off as a result. His volunteer coordinator job was taken on by two volunteer staff, who later became low-paid personnel through the University's work-study program and the government Program for Local Service.

Seattle Counseling Service did not accept the budget cutbacks and was busy investigating the established procedures for redress. In January 1976 SCS went over the head of the KCBMH and had a hearing before the King County Council, the top decision-making body of King County. KCBMH presented the argument that they had $200,000 less for 1976 than for 1975 and were under a State directive to prioritize funding for the seriously.disturbed. The KCBMH claimed that Funding for other programs, i.e. the public health nurses and the Asian Counseling Service were reduced. Documents submitted included Board Review Committee materials, SCS' hearing materials before KCBMH, and letters regarding SCS funding and the Board's intention to reduce it. The argument was made that funding was intended to go to community mental health centers and not tosplintered delivery systems. delivery systems.

The SCS presentation had two parts. One part consisted of an item-by-item recounting of correspondence and communications. The other part consisted of the following:
1. statements and statistics on the sexual minority population;
2. a statement of SCS rationale for existence;
3. service statistics with a year-to-year growth chart and statistics indicating a 60% correlation with County priority funding categories, besides the issue of an additional County commitment of 10% funding for "specialized minority programs";
4. a statement concerning SCS integration into the larger mental health system;
5. a statement referring to the County commitment to fund agencies at their present level of funding and the policy that changes were to be made on an across-the-board basis;
6. statistics showing the low cost per client at SCS, and posing the question of County plans for dealing with sexual minorities through other means at a higher cost should SCS be discontinued.

It was finally charged that the differential treatment of SCS in comparison with other agencies was discriminatory; and SCS requested that the $2,916 denied for the latter half of 1975 and full funding for 1976 be restored.

The Council set up a second hearing of the case for February to ascertain whether SCS had in fact been treated differently than other County-funded agencies. At that hearing SCS presented material showing the following:

1. that SCS alone had had a funding cut;
2. that there was an increase rather than a decrease in the total money figure available for 1976 over 1975; and
3. that three other programs' funding levels were increased, including that of the Asian Counseling Service.

It was argued that SCS funding had gone beyond the seed money stage, since it had been funded from 1971; and that its proportion of money from sources other than the County equaled or surpassed that of the other agencies. The statement concluded:

> There seems to be no apparent reason why SCS should be singled out to receive a constantly decreasing share of public funds. We cannot help but question what are the real reasons for continuing attempts to squeeze out SCS.

At the February King County Council meeting, the SCS case was innocuously referred to as "Item 27." Funding was restored, albeit with a 30% continuing cutback ($6,085 instead of $9,714). The charge of discrimination was dropped from the County record. Nevertheless, SCS celebrated this decision as a victory.

Meanwhile the contract for 1976 had arrived in January. It was forty-five pages long and much more involved than previous ones. It specified everything, including specific record-keeping forms to be used; compliance with the King County Mental Health Plan and Washington Administrative

Code, a compendium of State regulations; priority client categories; monthly activity report, audits and inspections; evaluation; grounds for termination of contract; subcontracting; funding alternative and future support; and indemnification, including types and amounts of insurance required. This last item, the new insurance requirement, was singled out for attention. SCS had to have insurance by February and no provision had been made for where the money would come from. SCS took a loan for the money and got the insurance.

In addition to the requested restoration of funds made at the Council hearing, a request was also made for joint planning by SCS, KCBMH, and other interested agencies on the long-term program for providing services to the sexual minority community. The KCBMH Budget Committee was considering a new fee-for-service system according to which County money would be allocated to the agencies. With its rising costs and limited budget, SCS was anxious to relate to the possibilities of this more equitable system of disbursement. A point system was developed whereby services to clients with certain characteristics would be rewarded monetarily. These client categories included the seriously disturbed, aged, youth, poor, and racial minority.

An SCS board member who also had become a KCBMH member and a member of the Budget Committee, presented a rationale for rewarding a point or two for a sexual minority client category based on the traditional repression and underservice this population had suffered in the mental health system. By providing a point for sexual minority clients, community mental health centers would be encouraged to treat this population. This would also help the funding situation of SCS, which of course, was serving many sexual minorities. The point proposal was adopted, but this fee-for-service system was never put into practice. Nevertheless, the established mental health system had been impacted by SCS.

Changing and increasingly standardized and demanding forms and procedures became a regular feature of state-county-agency relations, with the direction of flow almost always in that sequence. Given the major emphasis on treatment of the seriously disturbed, the State formulated and reformulated definitions of level of disturbance. Each client in all County funded agencies was now classified in one of five ratings to indicate their level of disturbance. Computerized, quarterly, statistical reports based on monthly reports submitted by each agency gave service and budget data for all the agencies.

In September 1976, in response to its increasing control, the federal government received a paper from the Directors of Community Mental Health Centers of King County titled, "Community Mental Health in Washington State: Issues and Concerns." The issues laid out were the following:

1. Control of the system — the erosion of local power by the State

The original rationale of the 1967 Washington State Community Health Services Act which followed the 1964 federal commitment to the community mental health system, was that people were better off staying in their communities than being institutionalized in a distant facility. Yet local control was being usurped by the State.

2. Integration of the system — policies that are often inconsistent and contradictory

The primary problem expressed here was that deinstitutionalizing the State Hospitals under the philosophy of local community mental health care was not backed up financially. Instead of the money following the patients into the communities, it was entirely withdrawn.

3. Balancing competing demands and needs

The argument made here was that providing services to high

priority categories leaves nothing to the mainstream citizenry while it isolates and stigmatizes the mentally ill.

4. The financial impoverishment of the system

The paper called for correction of a financial base described as "insufficient, unreliable, and constantly in jeopardy." Indeed, Washington State had come to have one of the lowest per capita expenditures for mental health in the nation.

As it turned out, SCS was the most disadvantaged agency within a disadvantaged system. It was also one of the "specialized service providers" with secondary status as compared to the "comprehensive service providers," which composed the above statement of issues and concerns. A "specialized" service provider" is defined as "a provider which provides a single service to a broad client population or multiple services to a specialized client group." A "comprehensive service provider" provides a minimum of four of the basic mental health services to a general client population.[4] Specialized agencies are funded "when it is demonstrated that the service being provided is not being provided by another provider in its service area and cannot presently be appropriately provided";[5] and the "specialized provider has a plan for tying its services to the comprehensive provider in its service area." Specialized service agencies of racial minorities and sexual minorities were second class citizens in terms of status, funding levels and commitment and could only exist in the system as long as a comprehensive provider was not providing those services.

The 1977 King County Mental Health Plan describes a system in which pre-specified kinds and number of services are contracted for each agency for a set amount of money. Service objectives are broken into categories of identification; intervention/stabilization; growth/sustenance; interdependence;

and prevention. Within these objectives, service numbers are also specified by blacks; other minorities; less than eighteen years of age; over sixty years of age; and individuals with a gross monthly income of less than $400.

Numbers of service units and numbers of clients were thus set for the agencies by the County. For SCS these figures were based on somewhat higher projected numbers from the actual 1975 service level. The amount of money specified was set at $17,244, or the same amount as for 1976. The agencies were asked to resubmit their annual budget proposals to be in line with the actual budget allotted to them.

In May 1977 a site visit had been conducted. The team was composed of two from the State Bureau of Mental Health, and two from the Division of Human Services, one of whom was a KCBMH representative and the other the KCBMH executive. They reviewed the records and programs and met with the bookkeeper. Obviously in comparison with the first site visit and evaluation, greater care was taken to do a more thorough job through evaluator selection, evaluation criteria, and a clearer, more formal report.

Their report covered the methodology of the evaluation and an overview of the program, and made the following remarks:

1. client records are not in compliance with the Washington Administrative Code;
2. staff qualifications may not meet WAC specifications;
3. more formal psychiatric consultation liaison and ongoing medical consultation are needed;
4. the clinical program is incomplete and not meeting WAC guidelines in relation to screening, referral, intake/evaluation, and there is a need for medical evaluation.

The following statement was also made in view of the fact that the agency management was under a new director:

> The staff of the Agency have been left with trying to resolve the conflicting demands of providing services on a grass roots basis to a select client population that is concerned about confidentiality while at the same time needing to provide professional clinical services of a mental health nature that will allow the Agency to be fully accountable to government funding sources. Staff fear that the professionalism of being a mental health agency will discredit the Agency as a resource for the gay community. This conflict must be seriously considered by the Board of Directors with a policy decision that will provide needed leadership for the Agency's staff.

> The State regulations which are not being met must be evaluated in terms of the Agency's present policies. Compliance with the State regulations will require a major shift in policy and resources for the Agency.

Based on this review, the KCBMH voted not to extend the SCS contract beyond its effective date of June 30, 1977, and to study other ways of providing service to sexual minorities. The then new director (the first of the two women directors of this period) appealed this decision and received the following response:

> The organizational and service program revisions as documented in your appeal are viewed as responsive and appropriate.

In August 1977, another site visit was done and a detailed report made, stating the following:

1.   "a genuine effort by the director to improve quality of service delivery";
2.   "... the Agency now is technically in compliance with the requirements of the WAC, although some areas of concern remain."

   a.   further improvements in the client record system;
   b.   part-time volunteer professional supervision and consultation is not good enough for the long haul;
   c.   services not delivered at SCS must be gotten from other agencies...and by November 1, SCS should have a formal agreement with an agency for psychiatric and/or medication evaluation for clients requiring such;
   d.   staff training programs are needed, especially for supervisory staff regarding severe disturbance.

It was recommended that the board of directors be made completely responsible for the Agency and that this be recorded in the by-laws and submitted to the County by November 1. Further funding was also made contingent on the recommendation that professional staff therapists and consultants resign from the board. At the KCBMH meeting, SCS was told it would be funded for the remainder of the year — if the money was available. SCS was told that there are still problems but that it was meeting the formal criteria, and that beyond that was "a question of taste." SCS passed even though KCBMH might have wished it hadn't. It was also noted that for the amount of money SCS got, the criteria used to judge it were the same as for agencies receiving a lot of money.

The next site visit occurred in May 1978 with the new acting director installed. The team was composed of four members from the Division of Human Services, two from the State Bureau of Mental Health, one from the State Department of Social and Health Services, and one representative from the KCBMH. The changing composition of the site team over time seems to reveal the increasing power of the State over the County and the increasing hierarchal bureaucracy of the mental health system. The site-visit report was qualitatively different from previous ones. SCS got an enthusiastically positive review, almost a rave review in comparison with former times:

> SCS is to be highly recommended for the extensive improvements in its clinical program.
>
> It is especially gratifying to note that our previous recommendations have been followed, and that so much has been done with so little funds. The quality of the clinical work now compares favorably to that of other mental health agencies.

Informal reports went so far as to indicate that SCS had become the darling of the Division of Human Services. SCS had arrived after a protracted uphill struggle and the stage was set for even further successes in 1986, when SCS would be accepted as a United Way member agency.

[1] This account is based on my experience in the whole series of events described and the perceptions of myself and other SCS personnel and friends of the Agency. Even though the events indicate problems that the establishment mental health system had with funding a sexual minority, alternative or separate agency, the author is not holding individuals culpable in this account. For whatever reasons the events and trends recounted occurred, mental health administrators and decision-makers were probably intending to carry out their roles as professionally as possible.

[2] Seattle was and is among the more progressive cities in the United States in giving protection to sexual minorities in the areas of employment and housing.

[3] An analysis of the relationship between SCS and KCBMH for the four periods of SCS development is contained in chapter 7.

[4] CETA was a federal job-creating program, for which unemployed and under-employed persons could qualify. Of course, some SCS staff members making around $150 to $400 per month qualified.

[5] The King County Mental Health Plan, 1977

[6] Ibid.

CHAPTER 7

"The use of diagnostic labels as devices for social control applies particularly to ambiguous cases and to persons who represent a problem for society."

— John Townsend

POLITICS,
BY EXAMPLE

olitical advocacy can be approached from many angles. Responding directly to the County's and State's requirements is only one avenue for involved participation with — and education of — the larger human services community. Other outreach ventures are possible through more voluntary and/or local affiliations. In the Seattle area, more than 170 organizations belonged to the Council of Planning Affiliates (COPA)[1] Associated[2] with United Way, which funds roughly 20% of the budgets of United Way agencies in King County, COPA has as its purpose:

- to advocate for improved health and welfare services;
- to oppose sexism, racism or other exploitation; and
- to identify interests and concerns based on community needs assessment.

In cooperation with the Citizen's Mental Health Advocacy Committee,[3] COPA sponsored a workshop on sexual minority mental health needs and services. The year was 1977. As a result of that workshop and a subsequent workshop at the

COPA annual meeting, a Task Force on Sexual/Genderal Minorities emerged. The COPA board of directors endorsed the Task Force and its charge: to study and make recommendations regarding sexual minority services.

One of the major approaches used in producing the Task Force Report was a questionnaire.[4] This needs assessment questionnaire was designed to assess agency awareness of sexual minorities and gather data about availability of services to this population in a non-threatening way. The questionnaire went to all 174 COPA and an additional 17 United Way members.[5]

Study findings were tabulated and analyzed. Three areas of concern were awareness, treatment, and relations with police. Conclusions in each of these areas were that some progress had been made but there was need for specific actions and programs to improve agency and police awareness and treatment of sexual minorities. The Task Force made recommendations in each of the areas to: improve agency and police policies and actions; conduct training for agency personnel and police officers; support and find private sources of funding for existing sexual minority agencies and those wishing to serve this population; sponsor a forum by COPA for nonprofit agency staff; and increase publicity for sexual minority services.

Analysis of the questionnaire responses as presented in the Report indicated the following:

1. Fifty-five (29%) of the agencies responded to the questionnaire, 47 (33.%) private agencies and 8 (18%) public agencies.

2. The majority of the respondents believed the question of sexual orientation was not applicable to the delivery of their services.

3.   A large majority of agencies, 37 (67%) of those responding indicated awareness of, and sensitivity to, sexual
minorities and 32 (58%) knowingly provided services to sexual minorities, although most of those had no way of identifying sexual attitudes.

4.   The vast majority of responding agencies had written personnel policies but very few included the concept of sexual
orientation.

5.   The majority of agencies provided for in-service training
of their personnel and a total of 37 agencies indicated they
would be interested in further education or consultation.

6.   A total of 25 (45%) of the respondents indicated they rated
their services to sexual minorities as excellent or good.

7.   Thirty-four (62%) of the agencies indicated awareness of
sexual minority services and indicated a total of 24 different
available services. Those agencies most known were Seattle
Counseling Service for Sexual Minorities, University
Y.W.C.A., Lesbian Resource Center, and Gay Community
Center.

A questionnaire-by-questionnaire content reading further
revealed that while the responses to categorical questions such
as "yes," "no," "somewhat," "excellent," "good," etc.
tended to be positively oriented toward agency awareness and
provision of services to sexual minorities, that some subtle
and sometimes not so subtle, statements in "comments" sec-
tions belied these responses.

As a result of its studies, the Task Force Report made the
following conclusions and recommendations in tables 1, 2,
and 3:

Table 1. Awareness of Services for Sexual Minorities

Conclusions:

A variety of special services for sexual minorities have evolved in recent years. Most of these agencies resulted from the lack of services in the wider community being made available on an open, accepting basis.

Evidence exists that antagonism continues to be encountered in the health and social services fields by sexual minority individuals seeking assistance.

Existing problems of sexual minorities require the continuation of effective outreach information and referral services. In addition, it must be recognized that sexual minority status carries with it a high risk of alcohol and other drug abuse.

Recommendations:

Existing primary sexual minority agencies be recognized and supported as necessary components of the community health and social welfare system. For the foreseeable future, they will continue to provide important services to individuals who otherwise may have no one to counsel with them regarding sexual confusion or sexual minority status.

Voluntary, private, and public sources of financing develop methods of funding organizations serving sexual minorities. Funding should be made available to primarily sexual minority agencies as well as those agencies desirous of expanding services to this population group.

Agencies which now serve, or make services available to sexual minorities, but which are not identified as sexual minority agencies, should clearly state their service and employment policies so the public is aware of those agencies as service alternatives.

Existing sexual minority agencies should expand their publicity regarding available information and referral services, education, consultation, and training.

Table 2. Treatment of Sexual Minorities when Receiving Service

Conclusions:

The majority of agencies indicated in the questionnaire that they are aware of sexual minorities and that their services are adequate. However, few agencies feel that minority status has anything to do with their service delivery. Also, only a few agencies have any statistics regarding sexual minorities or include any reference to sexual minorities in their personnel policies or staff assignments.

The Task Force heard evidence that, in fact, sexual minorities are often treated with disrespect and discriminated against in their receipt of health and social welfare services.

Recommendations:

All health and social welfare organizations reassess their operating policies, procedures, and staff training to ensure that sexual minorities are accorded services on the basis of need and in an acceptable fashion without regard to their sexual minority status.

The Council of Planning Affiliates sponsor a forum directed toward voluntary social agencies to explore the legal and social ramifications of service to, and employment of, sexual minorities.

The Council of Planning Affiliates cooperate with sexual minority service agencies, to the extent possible, in the maintenance of a coordinating mechanism to provide ongoing monitoring of service delivery.

Finally, the Council of Planning Affiliates disseminate this report in the widest possible manner to the various levels of government, health and social welfare agencies, and the newspapers, radio, and television.

Table 3. Relationship of Sexual Minorities with Police

Conclusions:
The relationship between the sexual minority community and the police department in Seattle, has improved in recent years. Both the police and representatives of sexual minority organizations have opened communication with one another. It appears, however, that further improvements can be made and those already developed must be expanded to law enforcement agencies throughout the State.

Recommendations:
All law enforcement agencies include sexual minority issues in both academic and in-service training programs and should routinely utilize sexual minority representatives to conduct that training.

This Report represents the participation of COPA, an other-than-gay, respectable community organization, in the issues and concerns of sexual minorities. It was a new and significant development. It spoke to the growing support for the sexual minority community and its service institutions and their recognized place within the larger human services community. While no specific follow-up was done on the COPA report, in 1985 SCS was awarded funded membership in United Way, with which COPA was affiliated and now is a part of the Funding and Allocations Department.

The counseling philosophy at SCS is one in which the client's sexual identity is not directed to be one way or another. A client-centered approach is characteristic.

Sexual orientation is viewed as the client's right and responsibility. The counselor's interest is in assisting the client to achieve their most happy and healthy sexual and life adjustment.

The counselors need not themselves be sexual minorities or have the same sexual identity as their clients. Counselors at SCS have been homosexual, heterosexual, bisexual, transsexual, and transvestite. All counselors are expected to be accepting and non-judgmental regarding these sex variations. Counselors and clients are matched for similar identities, sex, age, and class background. Alongside professional background, the peer counseling model is seen as contributing to interaction effectiveness from a therapeutic standpoint.

People classify, categorize, then communicate and interact based on their perceptions of reality. Cognition, the processing of perception, has a cultural component.

Many studies have shown that the cognitive similarities or differences between therapist and client have definite impact on therapy.

Dr. John Carr has tested the effects of cognitive similarities/differences in patient-therapist interactions. He found that patient-therapist similarity, especially the "therapists' ability to accurately perceive and communicate within the system of cognitive dimensions which comprise the patients' conceptualization of experience"[6] is positively related to therapeutic success. His literature review[7] indicates that some researchers have found difficulties between white therapists and black clients; other researchers have not found this to be the case. In an unpublished study, Dr. Carr and Dr. Marsha Gadd have found that client-therapist cognitive similarity is more important than race and the most important factor predicting successful interaction.[8]

The connection between and relevance of the concepts of "cognitive similarity" and the concept "explanatory model" is that what we are talking about is cognitive similarity in explanatory model regarding sexual minorities. When the

143

counselor and the client have cognitive similarity in their explanatory model regarding sexual minorities, they are likely to experience therapeutic success in their interaction.

Explanatory Model is a concept used by Dr. Arthur Kleinman.[9] It means concepts people have to explain "illness." Dr. Kleinman uses the EM to operationalize culture. By discerning the explanatory models[10] for illness of the therapist and the patient, it is possible to get at the similarities and differences between them. The EM can be used for discovering differences which are culturally (or subculturally) based as distinguished from individually based. It gets at the cultural belief system.

The concept of "explanatory model" can be used to refer to the concepts people have about sexual minorities.[11] The background which lies behind the political acts of COPA and SCS's "guiding principles" constitutes an "explanatory model (EM)." SCS' "guiding principles" are for a collective and subculturally inferred EM — which when applied to client-therapist interaction in counseling sexual minorities — can result in an optimum therapeutic experience. This explanatory model can usefully be taught to non-sexual minority therapists — so that they can more effectively counsel sexual minorities.

The author has inferred the following "guiding principles" of Seattle Counseling Service. Some of this is inferred from policy and structure. Otherwise, the author learned it as an explanatory model while working at SCS. It is what SCS offers clients at an organization with this EM — perspective and understanding about sexual minorities — and what helps them in counseling. It is also a political statement, a stance on sexual minorities which departs from that of the traditional culture's.

The guiding principles are:

1. that one can be a sexual minority person and be happy and healthy;

2. that one's sexual identity and adjustment is one aspect of a person's overall mental health and not the determinant of it; and

3. that counseling should be supportive and non-judgmental regarding sexual identity.

The explanatory model approach can be used in any client-therapist, patient-doctor, employee-employer, student-teacher, mentee-mentor situation. It is especially useful in situations in which the client and practitioner are sufficiently different to not be knowledgeable about each other's cultural conceptions. This applies especially to non-minority therapists working with minority subcultures, including ethnic/racial and sexual minorities. Therapists/practitioners can and do[12] ask questions in order to discover the EMs of the minority client. Information on client and therapist differences can help identify potential problems which would, in turn, be anticipated, and acted on. Both labeling and cognitive approaches lead us to infer that when heterosexual therapists reinforce negative stereotypic views of homosexuality, the results will predict the problems they anticipate. When sexual minority therapists and those nonsexual minority therapists do not reinforce stereotypic views, the outcome will reverse the problem.

The following detailed discussion of SCS organization and structure will shed light on boundary-setting — how it occurs and changes over time. When working with a stigmatized minority, the evolution of political process demonstrates boundary-setting. It speaks to who holds the conch in an organization.

The formal policy of Seattle Counseling Service is found in the following sources: 1) official documents registered with the State—the Articles of Incorporation and By-Laws; 2) SCS purpose, policy and guidelines documents, and decisions by the board of directors; 3) the Washington State Administrative Code; and 4) King County documents, including the annual King County Mental Health Plan, yearly contracts and other County-Agency communications.

In the Articles of Incorporation the purpose of SCS is defined:

> ...to aid, assist, counsel, direct and guide all persons seeking services because of emotional, psychological, social, psychiatric or other personal difficulties needing professional care and attention of medical or other social services. In addition the corporation shall attempt to educate professionals and non-professionals in the fields of social service to the problems of sexual minorities.[13]

By-laws changes occurred more often and were more intricately related to ongoing concerns of the Service itself. The areas changed have to do with membership, the corporation, board of directors, and the amendment of by-laws.

According to the by-laws of June 1973, the corporation is composed of voting members and non-voting, and supportive members authorized by the board of directors. Voting members are defined as:

Anyone who works with the organization on a regular basis or who has a defined role and title within the organization...[including]...the individual members of the board of directors and the individual officers of the corporation.

In the December 1975 by-laws definition of voting members, a distinction was made between the members of the board and officers of the corporation who are "indisputable" members and possible disputed members whose membership was then determined by a vote of the indisputable membership.

This distinction arose out of a situation in which some individuals from the gay community who were not in a defined role at SCS attended an annual membership meeting and criticized it. Staff felt that outside "agitators" in great enough numbers could be disruptive[14] or take over, since the ultimate power over SCS resided in the voting membership of the corporation. They elected the board of directors and could overrule a board decision by a two-thirds vote.

The power base shifted as the organization became more hierarchical and King County required that the board of directors have ultimate authority. While in 1973 by-laws allowed members of the corporation to be directors, the 1977 by-laws required that the two groups be separate. Now a member had to present the board with a request and cause for removal of a director. In 1975 and again in 1977, King County stated that the board must be the responsible, authoritative body of SCS.

At the 1973 annual meeting of the corporation there was discussion of election of a new board of directors, a nominating committee, and ideas for bringing on new members. Much of the meeting was taken up with defining the nature of the board, whose purpose at that time was conceived of as carrying out the will of the larger membership.[15] The atmosphere

147

was one of uncertainty and confusion. The board had only met once during the year and was uncertain of itself. The working collective effectively set policy.

By 1979 the annual meeting was combined with a board of directors meeting. The board was a working board aware of its power at SCS. Some of the people present at the meeting wondered whether they had a right to speak on SCS policy.

At the annual meeting and annual retreat, questions of agency evaluation, direction, and priorities were discussed. This was often an occasion for some controversy and community members to voice their views and criticisms.

One of the problems recurrently discussed at the retreat was the provision of services to the sexual minority population, regardless of class and political factions, the old, young, women and racial minorities. How to deal with inadequate funding was another issue. Problems of grave concern were: organizational efficiency of operation and volunteer staff satisfaction.

Two other items of note are a 1978 policy statement and a 1979 personnel policy manual, which laid out policy and personnel in detail. Much of these documents came from previously existing "oral law" committed to writing. They were expansions and elaborations of former policies, and part of the trend toward a more standardized, bureaucratized agency.

While the organizational structure of SCS changed, there was structural consistency from functional and service delivery standpoints. The basic structure consists of the board of directors and the membership of the corporation, which deals with policy and legal status; and a director and staff responsible for service delivery and day-to-day operations. An advisory board existed in the early period rather than a board of directors. An advisory board additional to the board of directors, was instituted in 1974 at the behest of the County and disbanded after a year as legally unnecessary, and it never had been functional.

During the early period a steering committee composed of the director, administrative staff, a representative from the advisory board, and sometimes others, ran the Service. The general staff had meetings, and there were low-paid positions with set tasks.

During the tripartite organization, there was a collective structure. Three small collectives each headed by a coordinator fed into the overall staff collective. The coordinators met as a sort of steering committee.

During the third and fourth periods there were board of directors, administrative staff, and volunteer staff. There were fixed personnel positions, the nature and organization of which fluctuated a good deal.

The creation and dissolution of personnel positions had historically been both internally induced and externally imposed. Instances were the transition from a director to tripartite coordinators and back to a director. The first transition was related to internal personnel and philosophical considerations, while the return to a director was externally mandated by the County as were the boards of directors and advisors. Once the director was in place, a more organized structure was instituted. The continued concern with structural changes was related to the desire and perceived need for increased organization and the external demands of the County.

Due to financial constraints and a philosophy of volunteerism, the staff has been primarily volunteer. During the early period, some low-paid staff salaries existed, both from SCS and government employee program sources. In the second period the director herself was full-time and unpaid.

The increased County grant toward the end of the tripartite organization allowed for minimal salaries to a larger group of workers. More regular salaries came into being in the third period and continued into the fourth due to three CETA positions. These salaries resulted in a structural division between the paid, administrative staff and the unpaid, volunteer staff. The paid staff became responsible for administration, programming, volunteer recruitment, training, and supervision. The unpaid staff did the bulk of the counseling although paid staff counseled too.

There have also been ad hoc and relatively short-lived committees. Committee membership had variously been composed of persons from any and all of the structures, e.g. board of directors, administrative staff, volunteer staff. Committees had been supervisory and evaluative, such as the program committee composed of board and administrative staff persons; task-oriented, such as nominations, financial, forms design and building search committees; or work party and event oriented, such as educationals, fund raisers, parties in honor of staff members, clean-up and fix-up.

Procedural matters changed repeatedly over the history of the Service and a point-by-point enumeration would be onerous. A number of attempts and some completed documents on procedural guidelines were done. The incomplete attempts related to the complexity and confusion of changing procedures in rather disorganized fashion. In the fourth period, procedural documents were required, focused on, and completed. The procedure became more organized and standardized.

In the fourth period in-person clients go through an initial intake interview (and pre-intake interview as well from 1985) covering: vital statistics, presenting problem, and medical evaluation. A GAS[16] level of disturbance rating is given. The client is referred to a counselor or program. The counselor works with a treatment plan, keeping session-by-session case management notes. Monthly progress evaluations are done as is a treatment termination summary. Counselors meet with a psychiatric consultant to review cases on an as-needed basis. The clinical director reviews the written client records, making sure they meet government requirements.

The issue of client confidentiality has always been important at SCS and is true for counseling generally. The added factor of stigma associated with sexual minorities has made confidentiality even more important. The reporting of client data to the government is done strictly by code with identifying data absent.

An in-depth case study of the Seattle Counseling Service for Sexual Minorities has examined its developmental history, guiding principles, structure, policy, procedure and services. Particular attention was given to its relations with the gay community in its diverse manifestations over time on the one hand, and its relations with the larger mental health system on the other hand, with the institution treading a tightrope between them. On the one hand SCS derives its support and credibility from the sexual minority community, and on the other hand, from the mental health system.

A marked difference in status and approach to relations with the government funding agent distinguished the first and fourth periods with their more professional mental health model, from the second and third periods. The first and fourth periods were conciliatory in relation to the governmental mental health system. The second period was ambivalent regarding funding, wanting the money and not the strings attached. The third period relationship was rocky and mistrustful and SCS' approach was confrontive and explicitly political. Although the challenges to maintain funding were met in all periods, the tenor of the relationship was markedly different. The government predictably preferred the conciliatory, professional mode over the confrontive, political mode.

The history of relations between SCS and KCBMH evidenced the former's long term struggle to maintain the relationship while the latter sought to dissolve it. The kinds of barriers the Service had to overcome and the character of the battle changed. The earlier attempts to cut off funds were done in an arbitrary, unsophisticated fashion. This was responded to by public confrontation at the 1974 KCBMH meeting and before the King County Council in 1976. Later KCBMH imposed increased regulations and terms of compliance. SCS had to meet the same regulations as mental health centers with many times greater budgets. Requirements for insurance, medical and psychiatric supervision, professional staffing and in-service training all had to be managed on a reduced budget in conditions of soaring inflation.

The relations between SCS and various sectors of the gay community fluctuated as well. In the first and fourth periods SCS was associated with the more moderate sector of the community, while in the second and third periods, SCS was influenced by two different, radical factions. The first faction expressed its politics in form, in the sense of acting out in manners contrary to acceptable societal norms, such as taunting drag dress. This was at the time of the more general countercultural movement in the United States. The second faction was radical in the sense of having a defined program for changing society to its roots through the revolution of women, workers, racial and sexual minorities.

SCS was the meeting ground between the lesbian/gay subculture and the mental health system representing the larger culture.

The nature of the periods and the approaches of SCS to its relations with the factions in the gay community and with KCBMH is represented as follows:

Gay Community	SCS	KCBMH
1. moderate	homophile	innovative, conciliatory
2. Radical, countercultureal	gay liberation	ambivalent
3. socialist-feminist	socialist	confrontive
4. moderate	professional	maintenance, conciliatory

The overall trend at SCS has been one toward increased institutionalization and bureaucracy. In the second period the motivation stated by the director for the specific development of records and communications systems was increasing client load and agency size. In the third and fourth periods the material incentive associated with the necessity for and development of a paid, administrative staff became the driving force behind compliance and maintenance of the connection with a bureaucratic governmental superstructure.

Seattle Counseling Service administrative staff in particular spent much of their energies on maintaining financial and personnel viability. The County funding source was insufficient and unstable and always in need of energy input to hold onto the funding, meet County demands and Washington Administrative Code regulations, keep up client records, do statistical and other kinds of reports, budgets, site visit preparation, and adapt to repeated changes in the system. The CETA positions were temporary and endangered on repeated occasions, resulting in strains on personnel and worry about agency survival should paid staff be laid off.[17] Other sources of support for personnel, such as work-study and Program for Local Service were time limited. Money from client fees and donations were unstable and not major sources. More effort is now put into collecting client fees than in former periods. Search and application for new sources of funding was ongoing. This included grant requests to private foundations, the City, repeated proposals to the County, etc. The results of these efforts were negligible until the fourth period. No foundation was willing to fund SCS, some for defensible and others for prejudicial reasons. The receipt of Title XIX funds for 1979 added another small increment dependent on client turnover and qualifications for this program. In the fourth period greater success in collecting client fees, government sources of funding, and acceptance into United Way occurred.

The tendency for increased institutionalization and conservatism occurring since the fourth period is in keeping with the theoretical propositions of Max Weber regarding organizational development toward ''bureaucratization'' and the ''routinization of charisma.'' Peter Blau wrote that the development of radical organizations out of institutions is not out of keeping with Weber's ideas:

> Notwithstanding his emphasis on the unrelenting forces of rationalization and bureaucratization, he also calls attention to the intermittent eruption of charismatic

leaders and movements, thereby contradicting the linear conception of change his other analysis seems to imply.[18]

We saw that although steps toward institutionalization were pursued by the second period director, and that she anticipated future movement in this direction, the subsequent period became more politically oriented, particularly through the influence of the director of the third period, who, however, was ultimately unable to sway and represent a followership. A political organization was spawned at this time from an educational series. SCS was in an initiating or facilitating role on more than one occasion by reason of being the most stable gay organization in the city on the one hand, and by being politically constrained through its connections with the government and Hatch Act on the other hand.

Despite the prevailing force of the material incentive, the purposive element of SCS remained intact. While the material incentive is associated with bureaucracy, the purposive element is associated with the social movement. SCS continued to fulfill its stated purpose of providing mental health services to sexual minorities and education to professionals and the public.

The political character and level of participation of SCS has changed. In the sense that the very existence of this alternative to the established mental health system for something that some have considered a sin, crime, or sickness is political, this element has remained intact as well.

---

[1] This number included: 60 United Way agencies, 70 private nonprofit agencies, and 44 public agencies.

[2] COPA was incorporated into the Planning and Allocations Department of United Way in 1980.

[3] The Mental Health Advocacy Group was a group of people who banded together for the original purpose of advocating changes in the legislation and funding of mental health services.

[4] The author designed the questionnaire with input from other members of the Task Force.

[5] COPA agencies are nonprofit organizations. United Way members are funded agencies meeting criteria such as age of the organization, board members, audited books, and proven service to the community.

[6] John Carr, "Differentiation Similarity of Patient and Therapist and the Outcome of Psychotherapy," Journal of Abnormal Psychology, Vol. 76, no. 3 (1970), 361-69

[7] John Carr and Allan Posthuma, "Differentiation Matching in Psychotherapy," Canadian Psychological Review, Vol. 16, no. 1 (January, 1975)

[8] Marsha Gadd and John Carr, unpublished manuscript, personal communication (Seattle: University of Washington, 1986)

[9] Dr. Arthur Kleinman is a prominent Medical Anthropologist and Psychiatrist formerly on the faculty at the University of Washington and currently at Harvard University.

[10] See the discussion of SCS' guiding principles coming up soon in this chapter.

[11] This is not to say that being gay is an illness. As an anthropoligist, the author considers the concept of explanatory model to be widely applicable.

[12] Experienced clients ask questions to potential therapists as well as vice versa.

[13] This purpose statement is differently worded than the purpose statement in the 1985 SCS Annual Report (see chapter 8 on SCS update). The latter emphasizes gay community health and needs.

[14] In retrospect, this protection against disruption from outside agitators had been unnecessary.

[15] This was 1973. In the intervening 13 years, there has been much work throughout the country on the purpose and management of non-profit boards; for example, the difference between policy-setting and advisory boards. SCS has learned and grown on its own.

[16] The GAS, General Adaptive Syndrome, was an assessment of level of disturbance required by the County and State, which were interested in prioritizing mental health services to the seriously disturbed client.

[17] Two of the three positions were lost late in 1978, one of which was able to be picked up through SCS money. While a 1979 proposal for four CETA outreach workers was granted, only three full time personnel remained to do basic administrative work.

[18] Peter Blau, "Critical Remarks on Weber's Theory of Authority," The American Political Science Review, Vol. 57, No. 2 (1963), 305-16

CHAPTER 8

"Institutional psychiatry fulfills a basic human need — to validate the self as good (normal) by invalidating the other as evil (mentally ill)."

— Thomas Szasz,

The Second Sin

QUESTIONS FOR
THE FUTURE

e have studied gay counseling services nationally and one service in depth. We examined their historical development, sociopolitical and economic issues, organization, staff and clients, relations with their gay communities and with the larger mental health system, results and raison d'etre. We traced their inception out of the gay and mental health movements and their increasing institutionalization in response to pressures from within and without.

We have studied one social-cultural institution in detail and wholistically, as if we were to have taken a plant, examined its roots, stems and flowering petals, the soil in which it grows, the air it breathes, the water that flows to it and the seeds that come from it.

We have attempted to apply ethnomedical, cognitive anthropological, and labeling theoretical approaches to the subject of sexual orientation. We have emphasized the significance of identity with and understanding of sexual minorities in client-therapist outcome.

Now we examine what we can conclude about mental health and culture from this study of a gay, subcultural, mental health institution.

We have seen that mental health is culturally defined, which is not to deny that there are biological factors involved in at least some mental illness. People in culture, not individuals alone, define who is sick and who is well. Conceptions of mental health and illness vary both from culture to culture and subculturally.

We have learned that when a culture labels members of a population as mentally ill who are self-disposed to view themselves as healthy, they can create a new cultural reality defining themselves as such.

Gay women and men have created a subculture in which they view themselves as healthy, and they have created counseling institutions to affirm and promote that health.

In so doing they have also impacted the larger cultural view of gay people. Gays have become agents of change — personally, socially, politically and culturally.

What do some (of the more enlightened) theorists write about questions of culture and illness, the medical system and homosexuality? Drs. Horacio Fabrega and Arthur Kleinman take the position that an ethnomedical model of mental health and illness is advisable. Fabrega has defined "ethnomedicine" as "the study of how members of different cultures think about disease and organize themselves toward medical treatment and social organization of treatment itself"[1] This concept is inclusive of that of "biomedicine," which is our "culturally specific perspective about what disease is, and how medical treatment should be pursued; and like other medical systems, biomedicine is an interpretation which 'makes sense' in light of cultural traditions and assumptions about reality."[2]

The biomedical approach is based on deviations and malfunctions of chemical and physiologic natures. Psychiatric disease has been problematic in medicine because it involves mental phenomena not directly observed and social behavior (Fabrega, 1975; Sarbin, 1969; Townsend, 1978).

Arthur Kleinman defined the concepts of "disease" and "illness." He defined disease as "a malfunctioning of biological and/or psychological processes" and "illness" as "the psychosocial experience and meaning of perceived disease...Illness is the shaping of disease into behavior and experience. It is created by personal, social, and cultural reactions to disease."[3] Additionally, whereas "disease affects the single individual, illness affects others as well."[4] Dr. Kleinman points out that the two may be difficult to distinguish or may exist independently of one another: Disease may occur without recognition that it is there. Illness may exist without disease, an example cited being hypochondriasis. Usually they occur, improve and worsen together, as in chronic disorders such as diabetes, asthma and schizophrenia.

Dr. Kleinman discussed the question of variable explanatory model with reference to disease, illness, and labeling theory. He wrote that what are called homosexuality, alcoholism and drug abuse, when interpreted from a psychiatric explanatory system, are:

> illnesses which may or may not be diseases depending upon whether the explanation used is derived from a psychoanalytic, biological, behavioral or social orientation. Interpreted from the sociological standpoint of labeling theory of deviance as an explanatory system, these are instances of social deviance that are labeled medical deviance or disease/illness solely for external cultural, social, political and economic reasons having nothing whatsoever to do with the "real" attributes of disease or illness.[5]

Some writers (Goffman, 1961; Scheff, 1966, 1967; Braginsky, et al, 1969; and Rosenhan, 1973) have viewed

disease as a means of social control. Fabrega wrote that powerful individuals and groups in the medical system determine
what is to "pass" as disease. They articulate the relevant norms
and definitions and prescribe types and levels of social control of disease for individuals who have it. These decisions
are based on social-cultural values and norms.

John Townsend pointed out that the use of diagnostic labels
as devices for social control applies particularly to ambiguous
cases and to persons who represent a problem for society. Some
of these categories are persons such as the poor, the unwanted,
the people who don't fit in. Talcott Parsons predicted that
medical definitions in the United States would be expanded
to include deviances. Pertinent examples are drug and alcohol
abuse, old age, and homosexuality.

Thomas Szasz traced the redefinition of homosexuality
through stages of being regarded as a sin, a crime, and a
sickness, first physical, then mental. Szasz views psychiatrists
as enforcers of middle class, cultural values, who label those
who deviate from them. John Honigman is also concerned that
psychiatrists represent middle class ideals:

> In dealing with a personality disorder, a diagnosti-
> cian may ask himself in which ready made disease
> category the symptoms fit; or (I now have in mind
> the existential psychiatrist) he can attempt to under-
> stand the disorder phenomenologically — from the
> inner world to which the patient oriented, the situa-
> tion he confronts, and the goals toward which he
> strives, whichever of these two diagnostic modes
> of approach dominates, the psychiatrist has reason
> to feel that there is something undesirable about the
> goals the patient pursues, the means he uses in striv-
> ing, the inordinately great or minuscule amount of

energy he expands in adaptation, his emotionally inappropriate tone of behavior, or the character of his relationship with other people. In one of more of these dimensions, the psychiatrist sees the patient as deviating from some ideal pattern which the psychiatrist leaves unvoiced. I don't question the value of psychiatric judgments arrived at professionally. I am concerned with their source and character as value judgments and with the consequences that follow.[6] Psychiatric judgments are value judgments made by some members of a class-divided society about other members.[7]

Culturally-based concepts of health and illness affect client perceptions of illness. John Townsend wrote that "...cultural conceptions do appear to influence patients' perceptions."[8]

Medical anthropologists have long been aware of alternative, folk medical beliefs and practices which coexist with the dominant cultural medical system in this and other countries. Dr. Noel Chrisman has commented on the significance of intra-cultural differences regarding health care conceptions.

Particularly salient intra-cultural variables affecting health care alternatives in the United States are ethnic, racial, class, sex, and sexual orientation.

Charles Kadushin discussed the dynamics of how various types of patients seek and get funneled into different types of psychiatric settings, hospitals and clinics.

Community mental health centers are often underutilized by minority populations. Yee and Lee wrote that:

Organized community groups, consumers of health services, and bilingual-bicultural mental health professionals have seriously challenged the appropriateness of the traditional mental health services for their respective cultural groups.[9]

The wave of alternative ethnic, racial minority, women's and sexual minority mental health services blanketing the country testifies to the use of alternative services to those of the dominant culture.

Data for gay males[10] indicates that a large percentage have seen a psychiatrist or psychologist regarding homosexuality. Martin Weinberg and Colin Williams found 43% and Joseph Harry and William DeVall found 41%. Charles Kadushin found 40% of the men under thirty-five years of age who lived alone or with a roommate who applied to a University Psychoanalytic Center in 1958-59 presented homosexual problems. Kadushin attributes this high percentage to word getting around that the Center was involved in a special research project with homosexuals.

Kadushin's reasoning here is supportive of his concept of the impact of what he calls the "Friends and Supporters of Psychotherapy." This concept refers to a loose network of individuals who support mental health-seeking[11] and contribute to awareness.

Such networking, awareness and utilization of mental health resources seems to exist at a high level among homosexuals. Probably multiple factors are involved in this. Kadushin finds that the young and the single are likely to present sexual problems, and that for married men, "youth, malehood, and

164

membership in the Friends override the fact of marriage and make such men as likely as the single to present sexual problems.'' He explained that:

> Membership in the Friends, aside from making talk about sex easier, also leads to pressures which produce sexual problems, for membership leads to a greater participation in the ''sexual revolution.''. Even if none of the practices of the hip crowd are in themselves emotionally injurious, they may conflict with the sexual mores persons learned as children. These conflicts alone may lead to the sophisticated person's feeling that he or she has sexual problems that ought to be taken to a psychiatrist.[12]

The cultural labeling of gays as mentally ill is another major factor accounting for the high percentage of mental health seeking by gays — whether they seek therapy on their own volition or through the gentle persuasion or coercion of others.

Noel Chrisman has discussed a theoretical model for the health-seeking process designed to accommodate the variation of such behavior in cultures and subcultures. This includes both popular, lay health beliefs and practices and folk beliefs and practices among particular subcultural groups. Like other subcultural minorities, lesbian/gay subculture(s) have distinct health-seeking patterns. There are intra-cultural differences too: gay women and men have different health needs. For example, gay men may seek a gay health clinic, public health or private hospital STD clinic in addition to mental health counseling for AIDS. Gay women may seek a women's health center for gynecologic care. Both gay women and men may tend to avoid establishment institutions and personnel in their health-seeking behavior, and are likely to use alternative services in the gay and women's communities.

Healing behavior can be applied to and have effects at cultural, subcultural and individual levels; these may be in conflict with one another. Dr. Kleinman wrote that when there is conflict between members of different health care provider systems, that:

> these may eventuate in patient non-compliance and dissatisfaction with the quality of care, misuse of available health care resources and culturally inappropriate care, as well as ineffective or noxious professional care[13]

With respect to the issue of quality of care, we have seen that lesbians and gay men have perceived their "care" in the culturally established mental health system as unsatisfactory, inappropriate, ineffective and noxious. Gays have been the brunt of crude attempts to "cure" them, when gays themselves have sought to be "healed."

Healing involves much more than cure of a supposed disease of homosexuality. Healing involves harmony of the individual within a social cultural or environmental context. Larry Dossey wrote about healing:

> Healing is not a matter of setting the molecules straight. It's a matter of helping the one in need of healing into an awareness of wholeness.[14]

The concepts of "harmony" and "healing" are key concepts in holistic medicine. According to holistic medical beliefs, humans are whole beings — physically, mentally, and spiritually — and interdependent with the rest of the environment. If something goes wrong in any part of the whole, the system as a whole (and this is also an axiom of systems theory) is affected. Illness can be initiated by or result from any part of the system.

The lesbian/gay subcultural context and the dynamic of being gay in a disapproving culture are definitely aspects that must be taken into account. Gays are likely to be "sick" in the larger cultural, homophobic environment and experience healing in the accepting lesbian/gay environment.

With regard to the issue of quality of care for sexual minorities, the question can be raised: How is inadequate funding related to quality of care? Furthermore, what else contributes? More money to buy the wrong kind of services would be counterproductive.

The following update on national gay counseling services is based on a small number of questionnaires returned to the author in 1986. Some notes about trends from these respondents follow:

1. The AIDS crisis has led to a mushrooming of attention and programs, and there has been some extra funding for this purpose. However, a quote from one respondent at the Pacific Center for Human Growth in San Francisco is revealing:

> While funding for AIDS is available for prevention, i.e. education, media, etc., funds for social services support for AIDS victims do **not** exist. As Dannemeyer said, "they're going to die anyway, why throw away money?"

2. The centers' relationships with their lesbian/gay communities continue to be vital and integral. Statements were

made indicating: more lesbians are being served, there is increasing visibility in the community, and that it is to this community that commitment lies.

3. The centers' relationships with the establishment mental health system have grown, including educational programs, joint committee work, formal and informal networking. The Gay and Lesbian Community Services Center of Hollywood stated it had moved from a "peer counseling" to "community-based mental health model."

4. Funding has increased, including sources of fee-for-service, donations, and government funding. However, the following statement was made:

> Our general services are still ignored by funders, government and private alike. We can't get needed funds for development, expansion or even maintenance of mental health services for the gay/lesbian community.

Seattle Counseling Service has had continued and growing success in recent years.[15] The Service has revised the agency purpose statement and aims to "foster community mental health" and "stay in touch with community needs."[16] The new director had been the clinical director for two years, and was installed as director in 1985. She has provided vibrant leadership. SCS has a strong board of directors and staff. SCS has remodeled its home, and strengthened its professional, volunteer and fiscal base.

Four contract therapists were hired and an adjunct psychiatrist is available for initial medical evaluation, prescriptions and diagnostics, and psychiatric consultation with staff. There were five (three full-time) staff, 30 clinical volunteers, and 25 crisis and referral volunteers in 1985. The board of directors reflects greater input from the business community than in the past, when there was more input from the non-profit sector. Business emphasizes legitimacy and respectability. The director is careful not to forget the grassroots and maintain a fine balance.

New program components include:
1. a pre-intake procedure;
2. a group therapy program among the first in the country dealing with same sex domestic violence and abusive anger;
3. the Basic Community Support and Treatment (BCST) program, which assists chronically mentally ill persons with living in the community; and
4. AIDS programs, which include: provision of a counseling component to AIDS pre-testing and post-testing at the Seattle Gay Clinic; the Worried Well group; counseling for relatives and friends of AIDS patients; and consultation to community AIDS organizations and private therapists.

In concert with Social Workers Northwest, SCS provides a roster of therapists with expertise in AIDS therapy and a contract with them to provide services to SCS clients with AIDS or ARC (AIDS-related condition).

SCS provides case management and financial support to AIDS contract therapists whose clients qualify for Federal Grant-in-Aid (SSI) and insurance.

Client statistics show that over 50% of the clients were coming to SCS for problems of depression (28%), sexual orientation (12%), self-esteem/self-concept (11%)(16% have presenting problems of self-esteem/self-concept), and sexual orientation exploration (30%). The nature of the problems indicates a need for an affirming, caring therapeutic environment. These clients would be devastated by blaming, prejudicial therapy.

SCS has demonstrated an abiding concern and sense of responsibility toward the mental health of all the sexual minority community regardless of sex, age, race, creed, national origin, or ability to pay.

In 1985 SCS received positive evaluation from the Department of Social and Health Services of Washington State for Title XIX certification. Its relationship with community agencies and institutions is good.

A breakthrough in the status of SCS as a gay counseling service occurred in 1985, when it received funding and became a member of the United Way. SCS is one of the first[17] gay agencies in the United States to receive United Way funding and membership. United Way is described as:

> ...an important ally in our work to provide top-quality mental health services to people in the sexual minority community and in our work for acceptance of the sexual minority community into the world at large. Our acceptance into United Way reflects the dream, work, and dedication of the people who created and developed SCS.[18]

The total budget for SCS in 1986 is $365,000, of which 4% ($15,000) is from United Way; 34% from a combination of government agencies: King County, State Grant-in-Aid (GAU medical coupons) administered through the County ($2000 per month), and Federal Grant-in-Aid (SSI CMP medical coupons, $3000-$4000 per year); 21% from client fees, 8% from fundraising, and 32% from contributions, including donated services.[19] This, in short, is a healthy budget, much larger than in past years and diversified in source.

The success of Seattle Counseling Service is not only measured in statistics, but in other ways, as demonstrated by two client vignettes:[20]

Audrey, a 32-year old lesbian woman, lost her lover, her job, and her apartment in one month. She came in for a one-to-one drop-in session with an Emergency Services counselor. She felt hopeless, depressed, and suicidal. Audrey also had started drinking again recently, after four years of sobriety. An emergency intake appointment was arranged, and the intake counselor took Audrey's complete psychosocial history. After reviewing Audrey's file, the Outpatient Services coordinator assigned her a primary therapist. Audrey has been working with her therapist for eight months and has resumed attendance at Alcoholics Anonymous meetings. She also uses Emergency Services counseling and the emergency phone line for greater support during times of crisis.

Carl, a 22 year old gay man and college dropout, came to SCS after being discharged from University Hospital two months ago, following his third suicide attempt. He is estranged from his extremely religious family, who rejected him when he "came out" to them last year. Carl is bright and articulate and shows no signs of psychosis, but he suffers from bouts of severe depression and guilt that seem to be triggered by episodes of sexual attraction to or contact with other men. He has a few friends, but none with whom he feels comfortable enough to talk about his sexual orientation. He wants to accept his gayness but feels overwhelmed by guilt in direct relation to his religious upbringing. Carl sees a primary therapist at SCS once a week and attends a "coming out" group at the agency. He has had no further thoughts of suicide and is beginning to express relief and gratitude at having a cohort of peers with whom he can openly probe his feelings about his sexual identity. He has also started to attend meetings and social functions of Parents and Friends of Lesbians and Gays, where he is finding a "family" that accepts him for himself. Carl hopes to resume his studies next year and, with his therapist, is exploring the possibility of enrolling in an out-of-state school as a way of establishing greater independence from his family and family values.

Quotes from the director talk about "the spirit at the heart of the Seattle Counseling Service" and "a strong thread of something precious here that's lasted over the years, something worth guarding and preserving." This is the feeling, the SCS tradition, the meaning fostered, protected and preserved by aware leadership, dedicated volunteers, a sense of impassioned, important work, and human caring which has been passed on over the years to those who come in contact with Seattle Counseling Service.

The following questions are derived from the author's knowledge, experience in the field while working at SCS, and conclusions. The questions are regular, ordinary questions — they are not new questions. The fact that these questions are applicable to sexual minorities, as well as to others, validates them. It also means that sexual minorities must be considered to be a population whose needs are taken into consideration for mental health services.

The questions mental health students, therapists, planners and administrators should be asking themselves are:

- How can equitable, quality mental health (and medical) services be provided for lesbians/gays?
- What kinds of services should there be and what should they look like?
- How should services be delivered?
- Who will deliver the services?
- How will providers receive adequate training in the lesbian/gay subculture, lifestyles, needs and issues?
- How should community mental health centers and hospitals interact with gay community mental health institutions
- What part of the pie should go to lesbian/gay community mental health services?
- On what bases should funding allocations be made?
- How should funds be administered and by whom?
- What qualifying guidelines and requirements should be met to provide professional standards of therapy and record-keeping?
- How much autonomy should lesbian/gay and other minority community institutions have in providing services to their communities?
- How should evaluation be done?
- Should any type(s) of service modalities (in-patient, emergency, out-patient, etc.) be required?
- How should consultation and communication between minority and larger system services and personnel be set up?
- How should education about sexual minorities to the broader public be carried out?

Mental health personnel should take these actions:

- Become educated about lesbians/gays and educate others.
- Hold staff discussions regarding information about and treatment of lesbians/gays.
- Become knowledgeable about lesbian/gay community resources, especially mental health services.
- Contact lesbian/gay mental health services for training, consultation and referral.
- Advocate for reform of legislation harmful to the mental health of sexual minorities.
- Be sensitive to lesbian/gay and other sexual minority issues among clients.
- Analyze client population to determine percentages of sexual minority clients in one's agency and make an estimate of the number that are probably in the area.
- Clearly state agency employment policies and hire lesbian/gay staff at all levels.

For students, therapists, administrators and planners, the following actions are suggested:

If you are a student read about and take one or more courses on sexual minorities. When it comes time to do work-study or an internship, consider working at a lesbian/gay counseling service.

If you are a therapist, educate yourself about sexual minorities. Recognize your limitations and proceed accordingly. This will include a self examination of the therapist's own sexuality, attitudes and beliefs. Learn to be open and nonjudgmental about sexual minority feelings and behavior in your clients.[21] If you find that your client's needs go beyond what you can provide, do not hesitate to made a referral or work together with a sexual minority therapist. Perhaps your client needs to know about lesbian/gay community resources with which to become involved; or needs to interact with other sexual minority people.

If you are an administrator or director of an agency, make sure your staff are educated and providing good service to sexual minorities. Find out if your agency's hiring practices are nondiscriminatory, and make it known in the community that you are open to hiring sexual minority staff. Find out how many sexual minorities are being seen and whether they are receiving satisfactory help. Set up a working relationship with a lesbian/gay mental health center.

If you are a mental health planner, meet with lesbian/gay mental health care providers and services personnel. Assess the mental health needs in the community and discuss what can be done to improve services.

If you are gay, you are an important resource for the mental health field and society. Whether or not you are or plan to be in the mental health field, you can provide personal testimony and education to non-gay mental health personnel. If you are a gay student, it's important that educational institutions open their doors to you and your interests in serving the lesbian/gay community — and that the community insist they do so. If you are gay and also in the mental health field, it is important for you to acknowledge this and to use your knowledge to help lesbian/gay clients; and get hired and help other gays to get hired as a gay worker in non-gay mental health settings.

While it is difficult to predict the future, let's paint two very different, possible scenarios, while fervently favoring the latter.

The bad news scenario is that a dark social, economic and political picture forebodes a worsening of conditions. Job layoffs of publicly supported positions, funding cutback and loss, governmental rule changes under conservative leadership, legislation and harassment by homophobes, might all play a part in wreaking havoc with lesbian/gay people's health and welfare and disassembling much needed services.

The good news scenario prophesies attainment of equality for gays and equal footing in society. This would do wonders for gay mental health.

Perhaps the ideal scenario would be a smorgasbord of services of integrated and specialized types. This would allow for different needs to be met and client choices to be made. Truly the conch would be distributed equitably among many hands — there would be many conches.

[1] Horacio Fabrega, "The Need for an Ethnomedical Science," Science, Vol. 189, No. 4207 (September 19, 1975), 969

[2] Ibid.

[3] Arthur Kleinman, Patients and Healers in the Context of Culture , An Exploration of the Borderline Between Anthropology, Medicine and Psychiatry (Berkeley: University of California Press, 1980), 72

[4] Ibid., 73

[5] Ibid., 74-75

[6] John Honigman, "Middle Class Values and Cross-Cultural Understanding," Culture Change, Mental Health and Poverty Lexington: University of Kentucky Press, 1969), 7-8

[7] Ibid., 8

[8] John Townsend, Cultural Conceptions and Mental Illness: A Comparison of Germany and America (Chicago: University of Chicago Press, 1978)

[9] Tina Yee and Richard Lee, "Based on Cultural Strengths, A School Primary Prevention Protection Program for Asian American Youth," Community Mental Health Journal, Vol. 13, No. 3 (1977), 239

[10] The author is unaware of comparable data for females.

[11] "Health-seeking" refers to the process by which appropriate health care from the perspective of the consumer is found.

[12] Charles Kadushin, Why People Go to Psychiatrists (New York: Atherton Press, 1969), 150

[13] Kleinman, 82

[14] Larry Dossey, Beyond Illness, Discovering the Experience of Health (Boulder, Colorado: New Science Library, 1984), 135

[15] The following information is based on an interview with the current director and information presented in the SCS 1985 Annual Report.

[16] Seattle Counseling Service for Sexual Minorities, Annual Report, 1985

[17] Another United Way agency is Seattle's Chemical Dependency Program.

[18] Seattle Counseling Service for Sexual Minorities, Annual Report, 1985

[19] These percentages are rounded off and the total comes to 99%.

[20] These client vignettes appear in the SCS Annual Report for 1985.

[21] Look for workshops in cross-cultural communication and health care...there aren't many. If there aren't the workshops you need, ask a community mental health center or university or agency or counseling center to set one up. You may contact the author, who does training and consultation on cross-cultural matters: "ethnotherapy" and "ethnomedicine."

APPENDIX A

SCS CLIENTS

This appendix provides statistics on client referral and client characteristics by sex, age, race, sexual identity, and presenting problems.

Clients get to Seattle Counseling Service in the following ways: self-referral, lay referral, and professional referral.[1]

Self-referral accounts for 28%, lay referral, including family and friends 36%, and professional referral 35%.

Means of Referral	% of Clients
self-referral	28%
friends	28%
counselor/doctor	12%
mental health agency	11%
family	8%
police/court	2%
other	11%

Table 11 shows client statistics by service modality over a ten-year period:

Table A-1. Client Statistics by Year and Service Modality

	A	B	C	D	E	F
1969	—	—	42	—	—	—
1970	2136	—	264	678	—	453
1971	3149	—	289	1264	—	2007
1972	4706	—	—	1260	—	—
1973	3489	—	227	961	—	—
1974	—	—	—	933	—	—
1975	17,500	—	—	—	—	1572
1976	—	—	330	2862	—	9968
1977	6491	—	259	584	—	4993
1978	6471	282	—	1555	35	1520
1979	5278	279	409	2052	90	347

Legend:

A	Phone clients	E	Number of family-marital
B	Drop-in clients		clients
C	Number of in-person clients	F	Group clients
D	In-person sessions attended	—	Indicates statistics not available.

As can readily be seen, client statistics are incomplete and vary in method of reportage from year to year.[2] These problems stem from a number of factors, internal to SCS and externally derived from changes in County reporting requirements and systems from year to year. Individual counseling has been variously reported as "service unit," "client hour," "client session," and "contact." "Family-marital" counseling is a relatively recent category. Finally, the accuracy of client statistical reportage is questionable. A major factor in this has been the reluctance which a largely volunteer staff have to recording counseling. Therefore, under-reporting occurs to some unknown extent.

Despite the aforementioned difficultires in statistical reportage of client services, this data indicates a general trend of growth of services during ten years of agency operation. While the numbers of clients vary by service modality in subsequent years, the general trend is upward.

Statistics in the recent period are much better than they were way back when. Some of the same problems of data reportage apply to the following statistics on client sex, age and race from 1970 through 1977. It can be seen that a similar pattern exists over the years. This pattern is one of a significantly high percentage of Caucasians, men, and persons between the ages of eighteen and sixty; there are significantly fewer non-whites, women, and persons under eighteen and over sixty years of age.

Table A-2. Client Statistics by Sex, Age, and Race

	1970 (%)	1971 (%)	1975 (%)	1976 (%)	1977 (%)	1978 (%)	1979 (%)	1980 (%)
Male	72	67	56	82	67	59.0	65.0	66
Female	28	33	31	18	21	29.0	35.0	34
0-16 yrs.	—	3	—	TG:	12	12.0	—	—
16-18 yrs.	2	17	8	5	3	1.0	4.0	1
18-30 yrs.	58	53	36	94	96	98.0	95.0	98
30-60 yrs.	30	26	7	1	1	1.0	1.0	1
60 plus yrs.	1	—	—	—	—	—	—	—
Unknown	9	1	4	—	—	—	—	—
Black	—	1	3	6.5	5	5.0	6.0	3
Asian	—	—	1	2	2	.5	2.0	2
Native American	—	3	1	2.5	3	3.0	.5	5
Hispanic	—	—	91	1.5	3	.5	2.0	—
Caucasian	—	81	—	75.5	83	90.0	89.0	90
Unknown	—	15	—	12	3	1.0	.5	—

— indicates no statistics available.
• In 1975 the age categories were reported as: 20-24, 25-44, and 45.65.
• In 1977 through 1980 the upper age category was 18-59 years.
• From 1972 to 1974 statistics were unavailable.

The majority of clients who seek services at Seattle Counseling Service for Sexual Minorities are sexual minority persons —lesbians, gay men, bisexuals, tanssexuals, and trasvestites. Client statistics on sexual identity are presented in Table A-3:

Table A-3. Client Statistics by Sexual Identity

	1977 (%)	1978 (%)	1979 (%)	1980 (%)	Mean (%)
Heterosexual	12	12	10	8	11
Homosexual	59	38	38	64	48
Bisexual	15	4	9	19	18
Transvestite	3	4	8	2	4
Transgenderal	—	9	10	1	7
Nonsexual	11	—	—	1	6
Unknown	—	33	15	5	17

— Indicates statistics not available

Clients present a variety of problems for counseling, classified into the following categories: Sexual orientation, interpersonal relationship, crisis, alcohol/drug abuse, emotion, coming as condition of other factors. The following table represents the numbers and percentages for the years 1970, 1973, and 1976 of clients presenting these problems and subcategories of them. Again, inconsistency in methods of data collection has resulted in inconsistency in specific problem category, reporting and numbers of clients (N). In 1970 N was 264, in 1973 N was 227, and in 1976 N was 127. In 1976 the method of reporting differed; it was a checklist format with the direction, "Check the areas you currently see as problems in your life." Thus, multiple items might be checked by any individual respondent.

Table A-4. Client Statistics of Presenting Problem

	1970	%	1973	%	1976	%
Sexual Orientation						
Homosexuality	—	—	24	19	31	24
Bisexuality	—	—	1	1	—	—
Other	—	—	2	1	8	6
Sexual Issues	—	—	15	12	65	51
Total	**73**	**28**	**37**	**33**	**104**	**81**
Gender Identity						
Transgenderalism	6	2	11	5	21	17
Transvestism	3	1	4	2	8	6
Total	**9**	**3**	**15**	**7**	**29**	**23**
Situational Problems						
Legal	6	2	—	—	13	10
Medical	10	4	—	—	14	11
Economic	24	9	8	4	48	28
Military/draft	8	3	2	1	1	1
Housing	—	—	—	—	5	4
Alienation/Loneliness	68	26	7	3	58	46
Total	**116**	**45**	**17**	**3**	**139**	**100**
Interpersonal Relations						
Family	—	—	7	3	19	15
Relationship	17	6	45	19	67	53
Total	**17**	**6**	**52**	**22**	**86**	**68**
Crisis						
Suicidal	10	4	8	4	26	21
Violence	—	—	1	1	11	9
Total	**10**	**4**	**9**	**5**	**37**	**30**
Alcohol/drug						
Alcohol	14	5	14	6	22	15
Drug	—	—	7	3	7	3
Total	**14**	**5**	**21**	**9**	**29**	**18**
Emotional						
Depression	—	—	9	4	54	43
Psychosis	—	—	3	1	—	—
Total	**—**	**—**	**12**	**5**	**54**	**43**
Coming as condition of:						
Hospital release	—	—	—	—	2	2
Court referral	—	—	1	1	—	—
Parole	—	—	—	—	4	3
Probation	—	—	—	—	4	3
Religious/moral	—	—	1	1	—	—
Total	**—**	**—**	**2**	**2**	**10**	**8**

— Indicates statistics not available

183

These figures[3] are for January 1 through August 30, 1980 for 167 individual, couple and group therapy clients:

Problem	%	N
Depression	12	20
Anxiety	4	10
Suspicion/paranoid	1	2
Grandiosity	1	2
Inappropriate affect/behavior	—	—
Negatism: denial of illness/obstancy	—	—
Danger to self or others	<1	1
Chemical abuse	6	10
Poor environment	4	7
Maturational	1	2
Social isolation	2	4
Situational crises	13	21
Marital roles	8	13
Parent/child roles	<1	1
Gender identity	4	7
Sexual orientation	16	27
Sexual functioning	2	4
Self-esteem/self-concept	20	33
Personal growth	—	—

Annually, an average of 27% of clients presented problems of sexual orientation; and 10% presented gender identity problems. This compares with 24% who presented emotional problems of depression and psychosis. Major categories are: interpersonal relationship (35%) and alienation/loneliness (25%), totalling 60%. Another major category is situational problems—economic, legal, medical, housing and military (40%). Other large categories are crisis—suicidal and violent (13%), and alcohol/drug abuse (9%).[4]

Rough as the statistics on presenting problems are, they indicate that a significant but minority of the problems dealt with at Seattle Counseling Service are solely related to sexual identity. This factor may add to or complicate the other problems, however. The majority of problems as presented by clients have to do with other-than-sexual identity issues.

---

[1] The referral data is based on 1977 intake forms which were used at SCS and standardized for all King County-funded agencies.

[2] This data covers ten years of agency operation. Despite the difficulties in statistical reportage of client services, this data indicates a general trend of growth of services during ten years of agency operation.

[3] Note that these are in medical model language whereas the previous statistics were in the language of self-reporting. This reflects changes in the direction of the Agency's growing relationship to the larger mental health system and its requirements for these categories.

[4] Alcohol/drug abuse are a large problem in the gay population. Another agency in Seattle specifically deals with it, which may reduce the number of such clients at SCS.

APPENDIX B
SCS CLIENT STUDY

This appendix presents results of a statistical study on client level of disturbance in relationship to factors of sex, sexual orientation, ethnic/racial background, employment, income, living situation, previous treatment and medication.

The data for this study was taken from Seattle Counseling Service 1977 intake forms. Although there were 277 intakes, 143 had data on level of disturbance. Of these, data on other factors which were incomplete reduced the numbers tested in specific instances.

Nonsignificant Measures of Association:

Sexual orientation, either homosexual or heterosexual, was not found to be significantly correlated with severity of client disturbance.

Sex was not significantly correlated with level of disturbance in testing for referral, medication, sexual orientation, living situation, income, employment status, and previous treatment.

Income was not significantly associated with severity of disturbance. What is apparent in this data is the large proportion of clients with low incomes at all levels of disturbance.

Living situation, eg. alone, with family, or with others, is not significantly correlated with severity of disturbance although there is a tendency in this direction.

Significant Measures of Association

It is significant at the .025 level (and at the .05 level for males) that "white" clients are less disturbed than "non-white" clients. "Non-whites" in this measure include Black, Asian, Spanish, and Jewish, although the preponderance of cases are male Blacks, Spanish, and Native Americans. Asians and Jews accounted for only three cases altogether and women for only three cases. Also, none of the Asians or Jews and none of the women evidenced a high level of disturbance.

It is significant at the greater than .001 level that those who hold jobs evidence less disturbance, or stated in the reverse, those who evidence greater disturbance, have less employment. Conversely, those with less disturbance are more often employed. Those without jobs in this measure include the unemployed and those on SSI, PA, VA, and DVR.

It is significant at the .05 level that persons with a history of previous treatment, which measure includes community mental health center, private counselor, and hospitalization, indicate a higher level of disturbance.

Interpretation of the Data

This study shows that sexual orientation is not significantly related to level of disturbance, while societally significant, sociological variables of class and race as well as mental health treatment variables are significant.

Minority racial status and low income are high risk categories for mental illness. One might speculate that an indication of higher level of disturbance among non-whites may be due to cultural barriers influencing diagnosis; it seems more likely that non-white clients are seeking treatment only when their level of disturbance is severe and that otherwise, they do not report for treatment at all. This may reflect a reality of life

188

or a cultural difference regarding attitudes toward mental health treatment. Cultural minorities may evidence health-seeking behavior which tends to preclude the dominant medico-mental health system in favor of folk remedies and indigenous healers. In contrast, whites may be more accustomed to seeking therapeutic intervention and less constrained by reality or life factors, such as the necessity of procuring food and shelter. Finally, treatment related factors, i.e. medication and previous treatment, are significant variables in association with level of disturbance.

APPENDIX C
NATIONAL CLIENTS

Nationally, gay counseling services evidence certain patterns in client characteristics, staff characteristics, client problems, and the kinds of services provided. These patterns are documented in the following tables.

The significance of the relationship of sex of staff members to sex of clients (see tables C-1 and C-2) is born out by Eromin Center, where women outnumber men as staff and clients. The St. Louis Women's Counseling Center is of course 100% women staff and clients.

dominated and lesbian separatists will generally not go to places which have men associated at all. The existence of separate women's and lesbian counseling services around the country demonstrates these phenomena.

Most staff members are gay (see table C-3), volunteer (see table C-4), and part-time workers (see table C-5). Other tables show professional status, training, and accountability of staff members (table C-6), client load (table C-7), client problems (table C-8), and service modality (table C-9).

In answer to the question, "What keeps you high," staff agree it is the positive services being provided to people. They feel the centers are used and appreciated in their gay communities. Some feel that some day gay counseling services may no longer be necessary while others feel the need will always exist. In any case, they keep on going.

Table C-1. Client Characteristics

	A	B	C	D	E	F	G	H	I	J	K	L
Women (%)	65	40	28	20	33⅓	45	10	—	—	45	55	100
Men (%)	35	60	72	80	66⅔	55	90	—	—	55	45	0
Age range	16-55	18-50	14-60	16-68	17-58	12-69	—	—	—	4-70	15-60	13-65
Average age range	25-30	20-35	25-35	35	23-32	20-30	—	30	—	22-33	25	23-33
Gay (%)	98	99	48	97	90	60	90	—	—	20	15	—
Transsexual (%)	—	—	14	1	7	—	—	—	—	1	—	—
Transvestite (%)	—	—	4	1		2	—	10	—	—	—	—
White (%)	93	95	83	85	90	75	75	—	—	80	—	98
Black (%)	7	5	9	5	9	10	10	—	—	20	—	2
Other (%)	1	—	8	10	1	15	15	—	—	—	—	—
% Paying	100	50	33	2	72	0	—	—	—	100	60	—
Non-paying	0	50	67	98	3	100	100	—	—	—	40	—
Third-party paying	—	—	—	—	25	—	—	—	—	—	—	—

Table C-2. Sex of Staff Members

	A	B	C	D	E	F	G	H	I	J	K	L
No. women	12	—	8	7	4	15	0	8	—	6	5	24
No. men	10	—	16	23	5	32	6	15	—	10	7	0

Legend:
— Statistics not available

A	Eromin Center	G	Pride
B	Identity House	H	Center for Social Services
C	Seattle Couns.	I	George Henry
D	Gay Community Service Ctr.	J	Chicago Couns. & Phsychotherapy
E	Persad	K	Neighborhood Couns.
F	Pacific	L	St. Louis Women's Couns. Ctr.

Table C-3. Sexual Orientation of Staff Members

	A	B	C	D	E	F	G	H	I	J	K	L
No. of gays	20	—	22	30	5	40	6	23	—	6	3	4
No. of non-gays	2	—	2	0	4	7	0	0	—	10	9	20

Table C-4. Volunteer or Paid Status of Staff Members

	A	B	C	D	E	F	G	H	I	J	K	L
No. of volunteers	18	All	17	29	8	45	6	23	—	0	0	—
No. of paid	4	0	7	1	1	2	0	0	—	16	10	—

Table C-5. Part- or Full-Time Status of Staff Members

	A	B	C	D	E	F	G	H	I	J	K	L
No. of part-time	20	All	20	29	7	—	6	—	—	12	2	24
No. of full-time	2	0	4	1	2	—	0	—	—	4	8	0

Legend:
— Statistics not available

A   Eromin Center
B   Identity House
C   Seattle Couns.
D   Gay Community Service Ctr.
E   Persad
F   Pacific

G   Pride
H   Center for Social Services
I   George Henry
J   Chicago Couns. & Phsychotherapy
K   Neighborhood Couns.
L   St. Louis Women's Couns. Ctr.

Table C-6. Professional Status, Training, Accountability of Staff Members

	A	B	C	D	E	F	G	H	I	J	K	L
Professional	16	50	13	1	7	27	2	—	—	16	8	—
Para-professional	6	60	34	3	2	20	0	—	—	—	—	—
Non-professional	—	5	—	25	—	0	4	—	—	—	—	—
Training program	no	yes	yes	yes	no	yes	yes	—	yes	yes	—	no
Accountability to clinical director	yes	yes	yes	no	yes	yes	yes	yes	no	no	yes	no
Supervision of counselors	yes	yes	yes	yes	yes	yes	yes	—	—	yes	yes	yes

Table C-7. Client Load

	A	B	C	D	E	F	G	H	I	J	K	L
Founded	—	1972	1969	1970	1972	1973	1975	—	—	1971	1974	—
Clients/year	1070	800	—	—	—	159	6900	80	2500	362	400	5000
Clients in first year	100	300	—	—	131	600	80	—	—	100	—	—
Active caseload	113	51	51	—	48	213	20	5-10	—	250	—	160
Clients/week	113	51	44	—	41	50-100	50	40-	125	70	—	

Legend:
— Statistics not available

A	Eromin Center	G	Pride
B	Identity House	H	Center for Social Services
C	Seattle Couns.	I	George Henry
D	Gay Community Service Ctr.	J	Chicago Couns. & Phsychotherapy
E	Persad	K	Neighborhood Couns.
F	Pacific	L	St. Louis Women's Couns. Ctr.

Table C-8. Client Problems

	A	B	C	D	E	F	G	H	I	J	K	L
Sexual orientation	40%	50%	—	25%	25%	55%	90%	40%	—	25%	—	—
Minor emotional problems	59%	45%	—	60%	65%	15%	40%	60%	—	25%	90%	—
Severe emotional problems	19%	5%	—	15%	10%	30%	refer	refer	—	30%	10%	—
Medication	no	no	no	no	no	no	no	no	—	no	no	—

Table C-9. Service Modality

	A	B	C	D	E	F	G	H	I	J	K	L
Individual	60	11	24	—	42	50-100	8	—	—	100	—	85
Couple	10	—	3	—	6	25	16	—	—	5	—	—
Group	15	25	21	—	0	500	—	—	—	15	8	80

Legend:
— Statistics not available

A	Eromin Center	G	Pride
B	Identity House	H	Center for Social Services
C	Seattle Couns.	I	George Henry
D	Gay Community Service Ctr.	J	Chicago Couns. & Phsychotherapy
E	Persad	K	Neighborhood Couns.
F	Pacific	L	St. Louis Women's Couns. Ctr.

APPENDIX D

QUESTIONNAIRES

NATIONAL GAY COUNSELING SERVICES

Date _____

Name of Agency _____

Mailing Address _____

City _____ State _____

Zip _____ Phone _____

When founded (beginning of actual operations?)

_____

Clients

How many clients do you see per year? _____

How many did you see in your first year of operation?

_____

How many clients are currently on your active caseload?

_____

How many clients do you see per week currently?

_____

Number of clients in individual counseling _____
Group _____ Couples _____ Family _____
Age range of clients _____
Average age range (10 yrs.) _____

Percentage of clients Female _____ Male _____
Percentage of clients White _____ Black _____
     Other racial minorities _____
Percentage of clients gay _____
Transsexual _____ TV _____ Other _____

Do you provide services for all of the above sexual minority
groups? _____
     If not, which ones? _____
_____

     Which others? _____
_____

Percentage of clients paying _____
Non-paying _____ Third party paying _____

Approximate number of clients seeking help with:
   Sexual orientation (acceptance, confusion, adjustment,
coming out, etc.)
_____

   Minor emotional problems (coping with stress, relationships,
mild depression or anxiety, etc.) _____
   Serious emotional problems (severe personality
disorders, psychoses, addiction, etc.)_____

Do you prescribe medication for clients? _____
   Who supervises medication? _____

Staff

Number of counselors/therapists _____

How many did you have when you started? _____

Number part time _____ full time _____
 Paid _____ volunteer _____

Number of professional _____ para-
 professional _____ non-professional _____

Number of staff women _____ men _____
 Gay _____ Non-gay _____

What training and/or experience do you consider essential
for a person to do counseling at your center?

_____

_____

_____

Do you have a training program? _____

Led by whom? _____

_____

Who must participate in this program?

_____

Do you have someone like a Clinical Director to whom
counselors are accountable for their work?

_____

Explain _____

_____

_____

_____

Are all counselors under supervision? _____
If not, what percentage are? _____
Explain which require supervision and which do not.

_____

_____

Do you have volunteer and/or paid persons on the staff who
do not function primarily as counselors? _____
What are their functions? (Describe the situation.)

_____

_____

_____

What modes of treatment do you provide?
Individual _____ Couples _____ Family _____
Group: Therapy group _____ C-R group _____
Other group _____

Do you have a specific approach to counseling (e.g., client
centered, TA, etc.?) Or do counselors use whatever approach
they are most comfortable with? Explain.

_____

_____

_____

Do you charge clients for services? _____
If you charge a flat fee, how much? _____
Do you have a sliding scale? If so, give the range.

_____

What other services do you provide besides counseling? (Educational, social, political, medical, other.) Which area is your main priority?
Briefly explain. _____

_____

_____

Please describe the administrative structure of your center, including board of Directors, administrative officers, division of responsibilities for various services, etc.

Are you incorporated? _____ Tax exempt? _____
If you have a Board of Directors, are they recruited from the gay movement, outside the movement, both? What kinds of people do you look for? Explain _____

_____

Are you affiliated with any other public or private medical or mental health system (or facility?) _____
Explain. _____

_____

What type of funding do you have? Please describe sources of income including grants, donations, fund-raisers, clients fees, etc.) and a little about the percentage of income each represents.

The following are questions about issues we feel are more important than statistics. We'd like to build our presentation upon those we find most interesting in terms of your responses. Since we can't afford lots of paper, copying and postage expenses, we'd appreciate your answering on some paper of your own and enclosing the answers with the two previous pages of printed questions with shorter answers. Your answers may be as brief or expansive as you like, but please make sure they include enough information for us to work with. Finally, please give the answers you feel best represent the values and attitudes of your center as a whole, as opposed to an individual feeling which may differ radically from that of other staff members.

1. Briefly describe how your center got started. (Why did you feel a need to exist? Did you grow out of the gay movement? Etc.)

2. What is the philosophy on which you base your service?

3. What problems have you had getting funded?

4. Are you accepted and/or respected by the "established" mental health care system in your area?

5. Do you care? (See #4)

6. Do other health and mental health care agencies use you as a referral? Often? Rarely? Explain why or why not.

7. Do you see yourself as part of the traditional or "establishment" mental health care system or as an alternative to that system?

8. If you are not a part of the established mental health care system, would you like to be? Why or why not?

9. What do you feel your impact has been on the gay community in your area? (Are you used? Appreciated? How do you measure your impact? Etc.)

10. What do you feel your impact has been on the non-gay community? (How have you made this impact? Educational or other out-reach? Etc.)

11. What do you feel your impact has been on the established mental health care system?

12. What is the extent of your educational and staff-development services outside your center?

13. What efforts have you made to attract groups other than those that comprise the bulk of your clientele? (E.g., racial minorities, low income people, other sexual minorities, etc.)

14. Are you feminists? (How important is this to you in terms of accepting staff persons, approach to counseling, etc.?)

15.   If your clientele is not approximately evenly balanced female and male, is this by design or default? If by design, why? If by default, what reason would you give as to why this is true?

16.   What is your position on the issue of non-gays counseling gays?

17.   What do you feel is your center's main problem at this point? Your best advantage? What keeps you high? Or worries you most?

18.   Can you keep going?

SCS CLIENT EVALUATION OF SERVICES

1. Today's Date _____ 2. Your Age _____
3. Your Yearly Income _____
4. What is your gender identity? Female _____
Male _____ Female to Male _____ Male to Female _____
Other _____ Don't Know _____
5. What is your sexual orientation?
Heterosexual _____ Homosexual _____
Bisexual _____ Asexual _____ Other _____
_____ Don't Know _____
6. How many sessions have you had at Seattle Counseling
Service? _____
7. Beginning with SCS and working backward (if appropriate), please indicate where and when you have received
counseling and rate those services (check):

A.   Name of agency or person _____

_____

Date(s) _____
Excellent _____ Good _____ Fair _____
Poor _____ Not Sure _____
B.   Name of agency or person _____

_____

Date(s) _____
Excellent _____ Good _____ Fair _____
Poor _____ Not Sure _____
C.   Name of agency or person _____

_____

Date(s) _____
Excellent _____ Good _____ Fair _____
Poor _____ Not Sure _____
D.   Name of agency or person _____

_____

Date(s) _____
Excellent _____ Good _____ Fair _____
Poor _____ Not Sure _____

8.   Please explain why you discontinued or were terminated at each of the above in order:
a)   _____
b)   _____
c)   _____
d)   _____

9.   Did you experience any problems in counseling based on your sex, sexual orientation or gender identity?
Yes _____ No _____ If yes, please state where and what was involved.
10.   Why did you seek services at SCS rather than elsewhere?

_____

11.   Please rate the services you have received at SCS:

FACILITIES: Excellent _____ Good _____
Fair _____ Poor _____ Not Sure _____
PERSONNEL: Excellent _____ Good _____
Fair _____ Poor _____ Not Sure _____
FEE: Excellent _____ Good _____
Fair _____ Poor _____ Not Sure _____
QUALITY OF COUNSELING: Excellent _____
Good _____ Fair _____ Poor _____ Not Sure _____
OVER-ALL: Excellent _____ Good _____
Fair _____ Poor _____ Not Sure _____
OTHER (_____)
Excellent _____ Good _____ Fair _____ Poor _____
Not Sure _____

12.   Please state any compliments, criticisms, or suggestions concerning the services provided by SCS.

_____
_____
_____

13.   Do you feel that SCS has helped you?
Yes _____ No _____ Somewhat _____ Not Sure _____
Comment: _____
_____
_____

14.   Do you perceive a need for mental health agencies specifically for sexual minorities? Yes _____ No _____
Comment: _____
_____
_____

15. Do you feel that sexual minority mental health agencies should be operated by sexual minority persons?
Totally _____ Partly _____ Not At All _____
Comment: _____

_____

16. Do you prefer professional or peer (similar to you and not necessarily degreed) counseling? Professional _____
Peer _____ Not Important _____
Comment: _____

_____

17. Would you prefer that sexual minority agencies be different from other mental health agencies in some way(s)?
Yes _____ No _____ If yes, in what way(s)?
Comment: _____

_____

18. Do you feel that sexual minority mental health agencies should be eliminated if and when sexual minorities receive equal rights and treatment? Yes _____ No _____
Doesn't Matter _____ Don't Know _____
Other _____
Comment: _____

_____

19. Would you like to see education about sexual minorities directed to sexual minorities? Yes _____ No _____
No Opinion _____
Comment: _____

_____

20.   Would you like to see education about sexual minorities directed to mental health agencies? Yes _____ No _____ No Opinion _____
Comment: _____

_____
_____

21.   Would you like to see education about sexual minorities directed to the community at large? Yes _____ No _____ No Opinion _____
Comment: _____

_____
_____

22.   Do you feel that sexual minority mental health agencies should be supported by governmental funding sources which fund other public counseling agencies (e.g., community mental health centers, Asian Counseling Service, Crisis Clinic) as well as SCS? Yes _____ No _____
Comment: _____

_____
_____

23.   Ultimately, who should be responsible for the funding of mental health services to sexual minorities? (Check one or more of the following):
A)   _____ All of society through government funding.
B)   _____ Interested people.
C)   _____ Persons who receive mental health services.
D)   _____ Sexual Minorities.
E)   _____ Other _____
Comment: _____

_____
_____

24.   If there is anything else you feel is important and would like to comment on, please do so.

COUNCIL OF PLANNING AFFILIATES
TASK FORCE ON SEXUAL MINORITIES

1. Please indicate type of organization:

Private, Not For Profit _____
Department Within _____
Government _____
Department Within _____

2. What is the purpose of your organization?

_____

_____

3. What types or service(s) or program(s) do you
provide?_____

_____

_____

4. Please describe the client population served annually to
broad areas (age, sex, race, economic levels) by program.

_____

_____

5. Does you agency identify sexual minority clients (homosexuals, lesbians, transsexuals, transvestites)?
Yes _____ No _____

6. Does your agency provide services to these people?
Often _____ Sometimes _____
Rarely _____ Don't know _____
Other _____

7. Please indicate programs or services provided to sexual minority persons (e.g.,counseling, social welfare service delivery, legal matters.) Please be specific regarding number of clients per program or service.

_____

_____

_____

8. If available, please give statistic(s) regarding your sexual minority clients (e.g., number, sex, orientation, gender identity.)

_____

_____

_____

9. Does your agency have written personnel policies?
Yes _____ No _____
Does the policy require the employment of, or service to, sexual minorities? Yes _____ No _____

10. Are there particular staff persons at your agency designated to deal with sexual minority clients?
Yes _____ No _____
If yes, please specify their number, sex, and in what capacity(ies) they serve:

_____
_____
_____

11. How would you rate your organization's service to sexual minorities? Please check one. Excellent _____
Good _____ Fair _____ Poor _____
Comment: _____
_____
_____

12. Please describe the staffing pattern of your organization.
Programs _____
Total No. Staff _____
No. Sex. Minority Staff _____
_____

13. Does your organization encourage in-service or supplementary training and education through workshops, retreats, released-time, etc.?
Yes _____ No _____ Don't know _____
Comments: _____
_____
_____

14.   Would your agency organization welcome education and/or consultation about sexual minorities in your organization?

Education _____ Consultation _____

Neither _____ Other _____

_____

Comment: _____

_____

_____

15.   Are you aware of services to sexual minorities in the Seattle/King County area? Yes _____ No _____ If yes, please list:

_____

_____

_____

16.   Do you make referrals or work cooperatively with any specifically sexual minority resource?

Yes _____ No _____

If yes, please state which one(s) and under what circumstances you do so:

_____

_____

_____

Agency Name   Address

_____   _____

Completed By   Phone

_____   _____

Please check if you would like to receive a copy of the completed Task Force Report. ☐

APPENDIX E
SELECT READING LIST

Back, Gloria, Are You Still My Mother? Are You Still My Family? New York, Warner Books, 1985

Borhek, Mary, Coming Out to Parents, A Two-Way Survival Guide for Lesbians and Gay Men and Their Parents, New York, Pilgrim Press, 1983

Clark, Don, Loving Someone Gay, New York, New American Library, 1977

De Cecco, John, Homophobia in American Society, Bashers, Baiters, Bigots, New York, Harrington Park Press, 1985

Fairchild, Betty and Nancy Hayward, Now That You Know, New York, Harcourt, Brace Jovanovich, Publishers, 1977

Gonsiorek, John, A Guide to Psychotherapy with Gay and Lesbian Clients, New York, Harrington Park Press, 1985

Griffin, Carolyn, Marian Wirth, and Arthur Wirth, Beyond Acceptance, Parents Talk About Their Experiences, Englewood Cliffs, Prentice-Hall, Inc. 1986

213

Hall, Marny, The Lavender Couch, A Consumer's Guide to Psychotherapy for Lesbians and Gay Men, Boston, Alyson Publications, Inc. 1985

Jullion, Jeanne, Long Way Home, The Odyssey of a Lesbian Mother and Her Children, Cleis Press, 1985

Martin, Del and Phyllis Lyon, Lesbian-Woman, San Francisco, Volcano Press, 1972

Reed, Paul, Facing It, A Novel of A.I.D.S., San Francisco, Gay Sunshine Press, 1984

Reid, John, The Best Little Boy in the World, New York, Ballantine Books, 1973, 1976

Scanzoni, Letha and Virginia Mollenkott, Is the Homosexual My Neighbor? Another Christian Viewpoint, San Francisco, Harper and Row, Publishers, 1978

Schulenburg, Joy, Gay Parenting, New York, Anchor Books, 1985

Silverstein, Charles, A Family Matter, A Parents' Guide to Homosexuality, New York, McGraw-Hill Book Company, 1977

Wolf, Deborah, The Lesbian Community, Berkeley, University of California Press, 1979

APPENDIX F

RESOURCE LIST

This is a listing taken from the Directory of Homosexual Organizations. The resources were classified under "Mental Health" and "Counseling." The list includes multi-purpose organizations that do counseling, e.g. gay student organizations, private practices, and professional organizations, in addition to specifically lesbian/gay counseling services such as were described in this book.

Androgyny Center, P.O. Box 31165, 220 N. Boylan Ave., Raleigh, North Carolina 27612, 919-848-0500

Atlanta Faerie Circle, 449 1/2 Moreland Avenue, N.E., Atlanta, GA 30307

Alternative Counseling Center, 38-42 Front St., Binghamton, NY 13906, 607-722-1836

Artemis Institute, P.O. Box 5642, Santa Fe, NM 87502, 505-983-3675

Association of Lesbian and Gay Psychologists, 210 5th Ave., New York, NY 10010

Battered/Abused Gays/Lesbians, P.O. Box 8141, Omaha, NE 68108, 402-345-5797

215

Center for Identity Development, 590 Valley Rd., Upper Montclair, NJ 07043, 201-449-0299

Chicago Counseling and Psychotherapy Center, 5711 S. Woodlawn Ave., Chicago, IL 60637, 312-684-1800

Cincinnati Gay Mental Health Professionals, P.O. Box 2934, Cincinnati, OH 45201, 513-421-7585, 251-5614

Community Counseling Center, 156 6th Ave. #229, New York, NY 10011, 212-807-9460

Community Resource Center/Grayline, P.O. Box 190835, Dallas, TX 75219, 214-368-6283

Counseling and Consulting Services, 161 Prospect Hill Street, Newport, RI 02840, 401-847-7229

Counseling Center for Sexual Minorities, P.O. Box 4852, Portland, OR 97208, 503-228-6785

Dallas Gay Alliance, P.O. Box 190712, 3920 Cedar Springs, Dallas, TX 75219, 214-528-4233

Foundation, P.O. Box 2264, Elkert, IN 46515, 219-293-8671

Gay and Lesbian and Bisexual Caucus, American Association of Sex Educators, Counselors and Therapists, 418 Elk St., Albany, NY 12206

Gay and Lesbian Community Service Center, 1213 N. Highland, Los Angeles 90038, 213-464-7400

Gay and Lesbian Community Services Center, P.O. Box 6333, San Bernardino, CA 92412, 714-824-7618

Gay and Lesbian Community Services Center of Orange County, Garden Grove Blvd, Suite E, Garden Grove, CA 92643, 714-534- 0862, 859-6482

Gay and Lesbian Counseling, 404 S. 8th St., Minneapolis, MN 55404, 612-340-7504.

Gay and Lesbian Counseling Service, 600 Washington, #219, Boston, MA 02136, 617-542-5188

Gay and Lesbian Horizons, P.O. Box 1319, 3225 Sheffield Ave., Chicago, IL 60690, 312-929-4357

Gay and Lesbian Switchboard, 1638 R St. N.W., Washington, DC 20009, 202-265-6495

Gay Peer Volunteers, P.O. Box U-5914, Tallahassee, FL 32313, 904-644-2003

Gay Rape Center, St. Vincent's Hospital, 153 W. 11th St., New York, NY 10011, 212-790-8068

George W. Henry Foundation, c/o Christ Church, 45 Church St., Hartford, CT 06103, 203-522-2646

Grow, P.O. Box 4535, Wilmington, NC 28406, 919-675-9222

Homosexual Community Counseling Center, 30 E 60th St., New York, NY 10022, 212-688-0628

Homosexual Information Center, 6758 Hollywood Blvd., #208, Hollywood, CA 90028, 213-464-8431

Homosexuals Intransigent, 446 W. 46th St., #1R, New York, NY 10036

Howard Brown Memorial Clinic, P.O. Box 14660, 2676 N. Halsted, Chicago, IL 60614, 312-975-9980

Human Sexuality Information and Counseling Service, University of North Carolina, Suite B, Box 40, Carolina Union O65-A, Chapel Hill, NC 27514, 919-962-5505

Identity House, 544 6th Ave., New York, NY 10011, 212-243-8181

Institute for Human Relations, 646 N. Michigan Ave., Chicago, IL 60614, 312-975-9980

Lesbian and Gay Community Services, 1010 Park Ave., Minneapolis, MN 55404, 612-371-0180

Lesbian and Gay Men's Counseling Collective, 406F Student Union, University of Massachusetts, Amherst, MA 01003, 413-545-2645

Lesbian Resource and Counseling Center, 2335 18th St. N.W., Washington, DC 20009, 202-332-5935

Men's Resource Center, 2306 S.E. Morrison St., Portland, OR 97208

Ninth Street Corner, 319 E. 9th St., New York, NY 10003, 212-228-5153

North Shore Community Mental Health Center, 47 Congress, Salem, OR 01970, 617-744-5322

Office of Alternative Lifestyle Concerns, Counseling Center, Mankato State University, Box 4, Mankato, MN 56001, 507-389-1455

Open Quest, 1305 S. Alvarado, Los Angeles, CA 90006, 213-664-5000

Operation Concern, 1875 Market, San Francisco, CA 94103, 415-626-7000

Pacific Center, P.O. Box 908, Telegraph Ave., Berkeley, CA 94701, 415-548-8283, 841-6224

Peer Counsel, P.O. Box 812, Santa Fe, NM 87501, 505-983-5598

Peer Services Hotline, P.O. Box 4035, Warren, OH 44482, 216-394-3253

Persad Center, 121 So. Highland Ave., 817 Pittsburgh, PA 15206, 412-441-0857

Phoenix Rising, 408 SW 2nd St., #407, Portland, OR 97204, 503-223-8299

Project Place, 32 Rutland St., Boston, MA 02118, 617-267-9150

Response of Suffolk Co., P.O. Box 300, Stony Brook, NY 11790, 516-751-7500

Sacramento Lesbian and Gay Mental Health Professionals, 820 24th, Sacramento, CA 95816, 916-484-1212

Seattle Counseling Service for Sexual Minorities, 1505 Broadway, Seattle, WA 98122, 206 329-8737, 329-8707

Sexual Identity Center, P.O. Box 3224, 2139 Kuhio Ave., -213, Honolulu, HI 96801, 808-926-1000

Seattle Institute for Sex Therapy, Education and Research, 100 N.E. 56th St., Seattle, WA 98105, 206-522-8588

Society for the Psychological Study of Lesbian and Gay Issues, APA, 1200 17th St. N.W., Washington, DC 20036, 202-955-7710

Student Health Society, c/o Hunter College Gay Community Center, 695 Park Ave., #124, New York, NY 10021, 212-570-5199

Unified Community Service Center, 2025 E. 10th St., Long Beach, CA 90804, 213-434-3089

We Care Center, Adelphi University, Ruth Harley Center, Garden City, NY 11530, 516-294-9834

Youth Environmental Services, 30 Broadway, Massapequa, NY 11758, 516-799-3000

Youth Health Services, 1918 1st Ave., New York, NY 10029, 212-360-7408

APPENDIX G
BIBLIOGRAPHY

Armon, Virginia, "Some Personality Variables in Overt Female Homosexuality," *Journal of Projective Techniques* 24:292-309, 1960

Arnold, David, A Process Model of Subcultures, The Sociology of Subcultures, Berkeley, The Glendessary Press, 1970

Barth, Frederick, Ethnic Groups and Boundaries, Boston, Little, Brown and Co., 1969

Bazell, Robert, "Health Radicals: Crusade to Shift Medical Power to the People," *Science* 173:506-9, 1971

Becker, Howard, "On Labeling Outsiders," The Interactionist Perspective, Earl Rubington and Martin Weinberg, eds., New York, Macmillan, 1968

Bell, Alan and Martin Weinberg, Homosexualities, A Study of Diversity Among Men and Women, New York, Institute for Sex Research, Simon and Schuster, 1978

Bene, Eva, "On the Genesis of Female Homosexuality," *British Journal of Psychiatry* III:815-821, 1965

Benedict, Ruth, "Anthropology and the Abnormal," *Journal of General Psychology* 10:59-80, 1934

Blackwood, Evelyn, The Many Faces of Homosexuality, Anthropological Approaches to Homosexual Behavior, New York, Harrington Park Press, 1986

Blau, Peter, "Critical Remarks on Weber's Theory of Authority," *The American Political Science Review* 57(2): 305-16, 1963

Blumer, Herbert, Social Movements. Studies in Social Movements: A Social Psychological Perspective, Barry McLaughlin, ed., New York, The Free Press, 1969

Braginsky, Benjamin, Dorothea Braginsky, and Kenneth King, Methods of Madness: The Mental Hospital as a Last Resort, New York, Holt, Rinehart and Winston, 1969

Bronski, Michael, Culture Clash: The Making of Gay Sensibility, South End Press, 1984, Boston

Brown, Howard, Familiar Faces Hidden Lives, The Story of Homosexual Men in America Today, New York, Harcourt Brace Jovanovich, 1976

Carr, John and Posthuma, "Differentiation Matching in Psychotherapy," *Canadian Psychological Review*, Vol. 16(1), January 1975

Carr, John, "Differentiation Similarity of Patient and Therapist and the Outcome of Psychotherapy," *Journal of Abnormal Psychology* 76(3)361-369, 1970

222

Carr, John and Allan Posthuma, "The Role of Cognitive Process in Social Interaction," *The International Journal of Social Psychiatry*, Vol. 21(3), July 1975

Carr, Michael, An Alternative to the Tyranny of Structurelessness: A Case Study in Organization Development and Human Relations Training, Master's Thesis, Leadership Institute of Spokane, Whitworth College, 1976

Cattell, Raymond and John H. Morony, "The Use of the 16PF in Distinguishing Homosexuals, Normals, and General Criminals," *Journal of Consulting Psychology* 26, 6:531-540, 1962

Cavin, Susan, Lesbian Origins, Ism Press, San Francisco, 1985

Chang, J. and J. Block, A Study of Identification in Male Homosexuals, New York, Anchor Books, 1985

Chrisman, Noel, "The Health Seeking Process: An Approach to the Natural History of Illness." *Culture, Medicine and Psychiatry* I:351-77, 1977

Chu, Franklin and Sharland Trotter, The Madness Establishment. New York, Grossman, 1974

C.O.P.A., Report of the Task Force on Sexual/Genderal Minorities, Council of Planning Affiliates, 1977

Darley, Philip, "Who Shall Hold the Conch? Some Thoughts on Community Control of Mental Health Programs." *Community Mental Health Journal* 10(2) :185-91, 1971

Dean, Robert B. and Harold Richardson, "Analysis of MMPI profiles of 40 College-Educated Overt Male Homosexuals." *Journal of Consulting Psychology* 28:483-486, 1964

Deforeest, Joan and Susan Vasbinder, "The Gay Community Counsels Itself," paper delivered to the Caucus of Gay Public Health Workers, 1976

Deforeest, Joan and Susan Vasbinder, "Why Gay Counseling Centers," paper delivered to the convention of the American Public Health Association, 1976

Deluca, Joseph, "The Structure of Homosexuality." *Journal of Projective Techniques and Personality Assessment* 30, 2:187-191, 1966

Deutsch, Helene, The Psychology of Women, Vol. 1. New York, Grune and Stratton, 1944

Doidge, W. and W. Holtzman, "Implications of Homosexuality Among Air Force Trainees." *Journal of Consulting Psychology* 24:9-13, 1960

Dossey, Larry, Beyond Illness, Discovering the Experience of Health, Boulder, New Science Library, 1984

Eliot, Thomas, Notes Toward the Definition of a Culture. New York, Harcourt Brace Jovanovich, 1949

Fabrega, Horacio Jr., "The Need for an Ethnomedical Science." *Science* 189 (4207):969-75, 1975

Gagnon, John and William Simon, Sexual Conduct. Hawthorne, Aldine Publishing Co., 1961

Goffman, Erving, Asylums; Essays on the Social Situation of Mental Patients and Other Inmates, Garden City, Anchor Books, 1961

Goldschmidt, Walter, Comparative Functionalism; An Essay in Anthropological Theory. Berkeley and Los Angeles, University of California Press, 1966

Gonsiorek, John, "Organizational and Staff Problems in Gay/Lesbian Mental Health Agencies," A Guide to Psychotherapy with Gay and Lesbian Clients, John Gonsiorek, ed., New York, Harrington Park Press, 1985

Gordon, Milton, "The Subsociety and Subculture." The Sociology of Subcultures, David Arnold, ed. Berkeley, Glendessary Press, 1970

GPO, Public Law 88-164, Community Mental Health Centers Act. Government Printing Office, 1963

Gundlach, Ralph and Bernard Riess, "Self and Sexual Identity in the Female: A Study of Female Homosexuals." New Directions in Mental Health, Vol. 1. Bernard R. Riess, ed. New York, Grune and Stratton, 1968

Gunnison, Foster, "The Homophile Movement in America." The Same Sex, Ralph Weltge, ed. New York, Pilgrim Press, 1969

Harris, Geophrey, "Sex Hormones, Brain Development and Brain Function," Endocrinology, 75:627-48, 1975

Harry, Joseph and William De Vall, The Social Organization of Gay Males. New York, Praeger Publishers, 1978

Hartner, Elizabeth, Lecture, Graduate School of Public Health, Pittsburgh, University of Pittsburgh, 1972

Hedblom, Jack, "The Female Homosexual: Social and Attitudinal Dimensions." The Homosexual Dialectic, Joseph McCaffrey, ed. Englewood Cliffs, Prentice-Hall, 1972

Honigman, John, "Middle Class Values and Cross-Cultural Understanding." Culture Change, Mental Health and Poverty, Joseph Finney, ed. Lexington, University of Kentucky Press, 1969

Hooker, Evelyn, "The Adjustment of the Male Overt Homosexual." *Journal of Projective Techniques* 21:18-31, 1957

Hooker, Evelyn, "The Homosexual Community." Sexual Deviance, John Gagnon and William Simon, eds. New York, Harper and Row, 1967

Hopkins, June, "The Lesbian Personality." *British Journal of Psychiatry* 115, 529:1433-1436, 1969

Humphreys, Laud, Out of the Closets: The Sociology of Homosexual Liberation. Englewood Cliffs, Prentice-Hall, 1972

Humphreys, Laud, Exodus and Identity: The Emerging Gay Culture. Gay Men, Martin Levine, ed. New York, Harper and Row, 1979

Jacobs, Sue-Ellen, "Doing It Our Way and Mostly for Our Own." *Human Organization* 33(4) :380-82, 1974

James, Jennifer, Ethnographic Semantic Approaches to the Study of an Urban Subculture: Streetwalkers. Ph.D. Dissertation, Seattle, University of Washington, 1970

Jay, Karla, "No Man's Land." Lavender Culture. Karla Jay and Allen Young, eds. New York, Jove/HBJ, 1979

Kadushin, Charles, Why People Go to Psychiatrists. New York, Atherton Press, 1969

Katz, Jonathan, Gay American History: Lesbians and Gay Men in the U.S.A., A Documentary. New York, Thomas Y. Crowell Co., 1976

Kay, Harvey, "Lesbian Relationships." *Sexual Behavior.* April, 1971

Kenyon, F. E., "Studies in Female Homosexuality — Psychological Test Results." *Journal Consulting Clinical Psychology* 32:510-13, 1968

King County, King County Mental Health Plan, Seattle, 1977

Kinsey, Alfred, Wardell Pomeroy, Clyde Martin, and Paul Gebhard, Sexual Behavior in the Human Female. Philadelphia, W. B. Saunders, 1953

Klaich, Dolores, Woman Plus Woman, Attitudes Towards Lesbianism. New York, Simon and Schuster, 1974

Kleinman, Arthur, Patients and Healers in the Context of Culture: An Exploration of the Borderline Between Anthropology, Medicine and Psychiatry. Berkeley and Los Angeles, University of California Press, 1980

Kraft-Ebing, Richard Von, Psychopathia Sexualis. Brooklyn, New York, Physicians and Surgeons Book Co., 1886

Landis, Judson, Sociology: Concepts and Characteristics. Belmont, Wadsworth, 1974

Lazerre, Arthur, "On the Job, Gay Doctors," Part 3, Seattle *Gay News*, Section 3, June 27, 1986, 49

Lewis, Oscar, "Culture of Poverty," La Vida, New York, Random House, 1966

Lewis, Sasha, Sunday's Women: A Report on Lesbian Life Today. Boston, Beacon Press, 1979

Liddicoat, R., "Untitled Article" *British Medical Journal.* pp. 1110-1111, 1957

Lockard, Denyse, "The Lesbian Community: An Anthropological Approach," The Many Faces of Homosexuality, Evelyn Blackwood, ed., New York, Harrington Park Press, 1986

Loney, Jan, "Background Factors, Sexual Experiences and Attitudes Toward Treatment in Two 'Normal' Homosexual Samples." *Journal of Consulting Clinical Psychology* 38:57-65, 1972

Malinowski, Bronislaw, A Scientific Theory of Culture. Chapel Hill, University of North Carolina Press, 1944

McNamara, John, "Communities and Control of Health Services." *Inquiry, A Journal of Medical Care Organization,* Provision and Financing: 9(3) :64-69, 1972

Mechanic, David, Mental Health and Social Policy. Englewood Cliffs, Prentice-Hall, 1969,1980

Merriam-Webster, New Collegiate Dictionary, 1975

Michels, Roberto, Political Parties. New York, The Free Press, 1949

Miller, William and Thomas Hannum, "Characteristics of Homosexually Involved Incarcerated Females." *Journal of Consulting Psychology* 30:193-198, 1966

Molohan, Kathryn, Richard Paton, and Michael Lambert, "An Extension of Barth's Concept of Ethnic Boundaries to Include Both Other Groups and Developmental Stage of Ethnic Groups." *Human Relations* 32(1):1-17, 1979

O'Donnell, Mary, "Lesbian Health Care: Issues and Literature," *Science for the People*, May/June, 1978, 8-19

Parsons, Talcott, The Social System. New York, The Free Press, 1951

Pauley, Ira, Adult Manifestations of Male Transsexualism and Sex Reassignment. Baltimore, Johns Hopkins Press, 1969

Rabin, Jack, Kathleen Keefe, Michael Burton, "Enhancing Services for Sexual Minority Clients: A Community Mental Health Approach," *Social Work,* Volume 31, No. 4 July through August 1986

Radcliffe-Brown, A. R., "On the Concept of Function in Social Science." *American Anthropologist* 37:394:402, 1935

Read, Kenneth, Other Voices: The Style of a Male Homosexual Tavern. Novato, Chandler and Sharp, 1980

Rosen, David, A Study of Female Homosexuality. Springfield, Illinois, Charles C. Thomas Publisher, 1974

Rosen, George, "The First Neighborhood Health Center Movement: Its Rise and Fall." *American Journal of Public Health*, 61:1620:37, 1971

Rosenhan, Stanford, "On Being Sane in Insane Places." *Science* 179:250-58, 1973

Saghir, Marcel, et al, "Homosexuality: IV. Psychiatric Disorders and Disability in the Male Homosexual." *American Journal of Psychiatry* 126, 8:1079-1086, 1970

Saghir, M. et al, "Homosexuality: IV. Psychiatric Disorders in the Female Homosexual." *American Journal of Psychiatry* 127, 2:147-154, 1970

Sarbin, Theodore, "The Scientific Status of the Mental Illness Metaphor." Changing Perspectives in Mental Illness, Stanley Plog and Robert Edgerton, eds. New York, Holt, Rinehart and Winston, 1969

Scheff, Thomas, Being Mentally Ill. Hawthorne, Aldine Publishing Co., 1966

Scheff, Thomas, Mental Illness and Social Processes, New York, Harper and Row, 1967

Scheffler, Linda, Help Thy Neighbor: How Counseling Works and When It Doesn't, New York, Grove Press, Inc., 1984

Schofield, M., Sociological Aspects of Homosexuality. New York, Little, Brown, 1966

Schwartz, Pepper, and Phillip Blumstein, "Lesbianism and Bisexuality." Sexual Deviance and Sexual Deviates, Erich Goode and Richard Troiden, eds. New York, William Morrow and Co., 1974

Siegelman, Marvin, "Adjustment of Homosexual and Heterosexual Women." *British Journal of Psychiatry* 120:477-481, 1972

Silverstein, Charles, A Family Matter, A Parents' Guide to Homosexuality, New York, McGraw-Hill Book Company, 1977

Szasz, Thomas, "The Myth of Mental Illness." *American Psychologist* 15:113-118, 1960

Szasz, Thomas, The Manufacture of Madness. New York, Harper and Row, 1970

Szasz, Thomas, The Second Sin, Anchor Books Garden City, 1974

Tennov, Dorothy, Psychotherapy, The Hazardous Cure, New York, Anchor Books, 1976

Thompson, Mark, "The Evolution of a Fairy: Toward a New Definition of Gay." *The Advocate*, June 26, 1980

Townsend, John, Cultural Conceptions and Mental Illness: A Comparison of Germany and America. Chicago, University of Chicago Press, 1978

Vine, Phyllis, Families in Pain: Children Siblings, Spouses and Parents of the Mentally Ill Speak Out, New York, Pantheon Books, 1982

Weber, Max, Essays in Sociology. New York Oxford University Press, 1946

Weinberg, Martin, and Colin Williams, Male Homosexuals: Their Problems and Adaptations. New York, Oxford University Press, 1974

Westphal, Carl, "Die Contrare Sexualempfindung, Symptom Eines Neuropathischen (Psychopathischen) Zustandes," *Archie fur Psychiatrie,* 1870

Wolf, Deborah, The Lesbian Community, Berkeley, University of California Press, 1979

Yee, Tina and Richard Lee, "Based on Cultural Strengths, A School Primary Prevention Program for Asian-American Youth," *Community Mental Health Journal*, 13(3):239-48, 1977

Yinger, Milton, "Contraculture and Subculture." The Sociology of Subcultures, David Arnold, ed. Berkely, Glendessary Press, 1970

Zald, Mayer and Roberta Ash, "Social Movement Organizations," *Journal of Social Forces* 44:327-41, 1966

For ordering information please write to:

Consultant Services Northwest, Inc.
839 N.E. 96th Street
Seattle, Washington 98115

or call:
(206) 524-1950